TORTURED SOUL

TORTURED SOUL
Jim Younger in His Own Words

MARLEY BRANT

TWODOT ®

GUILFORD, CONNECTICUT
HELENA, MONTANA

A · T W O D O T® · B O O K
An imprint and registered trademark of The Rowman & Littlefield Publishing Group, Inc.
4501 Forbes Blvd., Ste. 200
Lanham, MD 20706
www.rowman.com

Distributed by NATIONAL BOOK NETWORK

British Library Cataloguing in Publication Information available

Library of Congress Cataloging-in-Publication Data
Names: Brant, Marley, author.
Title: Tortured soul : Jim Younger in his own words / Marley Brant.
  Other titles: Jim Younger in his own words
Description: Guilford, Connecticut : TwoDot, [2021] | Includes
  bibliographical references and index.
Identifiers: LCCN 2020054640 (print) | LCCN 2020054641 (ebook) | ISBN
  9781493057122 (cloth : alk. paper) | ISBN 9781493057139 (electronic)
Subjects: LCSH: Younger, James, 1848–1902—Correspondence. | McNeill,
  Cora—Correspondence. | Younger, Cole, 1844–1916. | Younger, Robert Ewing,
  1853–1889. | Younger family. | West (U.S.)—History—1860–1890. | Outlaws—West
  (U.S.)—Correspondence. | Outlaws—West (U.S.)—Biography. | Missouri—Biography. |
  Minnesota—Biography.
Classification: LCC F594.Y77 B73 2021 (print) | LCC F594.Y77 (ebook) |
  DDC 977.8/03092—dc23
LC record available at https://lccn.loc.gov/2020054640
LC ebook record available at https://lccn.loc.gov/2020054641

Contents

Acknowledgments

As with all of my books on the younger brothers and the James-Younger Gang, I owe a huge amount of gratitude to so many people for taking the time to share their knowledge, memories, printed materials, stories, and documents with me. I have been studying these larger-than-life characters for over forty years now and have met hundreds of people who create a cast of characters in their own right. But my thirst for the true story originated with two highly intelligent and wonderfully insightful historians whom I am proud to call friends: Milt Perry and Dr. Bill Settle. The hours spent seeking facts, dissecting folklore, forging new and expanding relationships, and exchanging theories with these two gentlemen have been some of the most enjoyable of my life. How I miss them both, both professionally and personally. This one—likely my last on the subject—is for you, guys.

I also need to acknowledge the folks at the various and innumerable historical societies and sites that assisted me in my research. Of special note are the Missouri State Archives, Minnesota Historical Society, and the State Historic Society of Missouri at Columbia.

Kind and accommodating individuals throughout the country shared so much with me about their ancestors, towns, historical events, and the oh-so-many stories the Younger name invoked. My heart is warmed by the priceless personal friendships that were forged with folks such as Monika Sklore, David Smith, Marjorie

Settle, Dreat Younger, Ruth Whipple, Wilbur Zink, Ethelrose Owens, Thelma and Betty Barr, Othor McLean, Bob McCubbin, Jim Ross, Phillip and Charlotte Steele, George Warfel, Jack Wymore, Ted Yeatman, Pat Brophy, Ed Bauman, Donna Rose Harrell, Mary Withrow Davidson, Milt Edmonson, Chris Edwards, LeAnis Fox, Jim Fmer, Dee Fozzard, John Mills, Leola Mayes, John Nicholson, Pat O'Brien, Chuck Parsons, Jeanne Ralston, Pam Banner, Mary and Norm Smith, Flossie Wiley, Nancy Samuelson, Leon Metz, WG Talley, Elmer Kelton, Jim Dullenty, Frank Younger, Gary Chillcoth, Armand de Gregorius, and all the good people at the Jesse James Farm & Museum over the years.

None of my work on the subject would be valid to me if not for the encouragement and friendship of the extended Younger family. Rooted in the "Show Me" state of Missouri, they needed to get to know me before they shared their stories with me and I greatly respect that. That so many of them became so much more than kind suppliers of information has been an extra special reward, and I treasure them.

My writing career wouldn't be possible without the love and support of "My Boys": husband Dave, son Tim, brother Willie, nephews John and William, and my pups Chachi and Rory (who keep me real). I was blessed with some pretty amazing aunts and uncles too (yes you, AJ). My biggest supporters from the get-go were my beautiful mom, Gladys Wall Olmstead, and the man who sparked this particular fire, my very special dad Red Olmstead.

Those who read my books are a treasure, and I thank each and every one of you. I hope you enjoy reading this final account . . .

INTRODUCTION

I BEGAN MY JOURNEY DOWN THE OUTLAW TRAIL IN 1980. A VERY odd series of events turned my interest in the Younger brothers into a passionate thirst for the facts surrounding their lives, both the years dedicated to outlawry and the years prior when they were the respected sons of a wealthy and venerable civil servant named Henry Washington Younger. At that time, there wasn't a lot of information about the Youngers. It was their partners in crime—Jesse and Frank James—who were placed first in the public's interest for over a hundred years. Uncovering the facts behind the Younger story was a ten-year project that took me to over twelve states, countless archives, courthouses, museums and historical societies, visits to each of the locations of their robberies and life events, and interaction with dozens of people who just might have information, a clue or a lead, including Younger and James family members. One of the people I met was Wilbur Zink of Appleton City, Missouri.

Wilbur was a Pearl Harbor veteran who owned a car dealership and was also a pastor. He was not a historian but rather a collector of historical items. He also held a personal connection to an important piece of Younger history. His grandfather David Crowder played into the story of the ill-fated Roscoe Gun battle, where John Younger—the lesser-known outlaw brother—had met his fate during an altercation with men working with the Pinkerton Agency to eliminate the James-Younger Gang. Wilbur made it his goal to learn as much as he could about the shootout, and he eventually wrote a booklet about the event. He enjoyed telling the story and was the guest speaker at many civic and club gatherings.

During my second visit with Wilbur, he graciously took me to the site of the confrontation and the locations that were integral to that fateful twenty-four hours in 1874. He asked if I was brave enough to travel into the backwoods of rural Monagaw Springs, Missouri, to climb into the brush and down into the cave that over-looked the Osage River, the site of the Youngers favorite "hide out." I was thrilled to say yes, I was. It was an experience I treasure to this day.

As Wilbur grew to know me and appreciate my dedication to unearthing the factual stories concerning the Youngers, he shared something with me. He said he was in possession of letters that were written by Jim Younger to his first love, Cora Lee McNeil. He claimed Cora's daughter, Edwynne Neill "Deedee" Deming Deane, had given the letters to him. Cora Lee McNeil was the daughter of Dr. D.C. McNeil and Elizabeth Wright. Cora died April 20, 1942, in Los Angeles. "Deedee" was the third of Cora Lee's children from her first marriage to E. J. Deming. Born October 24, 1889, Deedee died in February 1976 in Banning, California.

Wilbur told me no one had ever seen the letters and that Ms. Deane had said that he wasn't to show them to anyone else. Regardless, on my third visit, he laid one of the letters on his desk in front of me, raised his eyebrows and left the room for a period of time. The document before me was Jim's description of his brother Bob. I quickly copied down the information and when Wilbur reen-tered the room, he smiled and took the document away. This was a solid piece of research for me and helped me on my way to further clues and historical data in my quest to better know the Younger brothers, Bob in particular. To my knowledge, Wilbur Zink never shared the letters he had in his possession with others, nor did he allow me a further look even though he knew I was writing what has come to be the definitive history of the Younger family. My book *The Outlaw Youngers: A Confederate Brotherhood* was published in 1992.

Sadly, Wilbur died in 2010. Years later, his outlaw collection came up for auction with the Heritage Auction house and I noticed with delight that many of the Jim Younger letters were available. I purchased the letters, anxious to find what other gems of Younger history they contained. Upon sorting through the file, I was surprised to see that it was Deedee Deane's request to Wilbur that the letters be published. After both their deaths, Cora Lee wanted the world to know of the love she shared with Jim Younger and felt the letters would shed light on the sensitive, complex, and dear man she knew Jim to be. In exchange for Wilbur's efforts on her behalf, Deedee gave Wilbur the violin that Jim had used to comfort and amuse him while serving his life sentence in the Stillwater Penitentiary. I was quite surprised that the letters were not to have been kept secret as I was told, but rather to have been made public by Wilbur. Why he chose to hold on to the letters and not share them remains a mystery to me.

Regardless of Wilbur's motive, the documents are now in my possession and they make for fascinating reading. (Since the time I obtained the letters, other letters have been made available through other auctions, but other than reestablishing the romance between Cora Lee and Jim they are not of the value as these.) The letters and recollections contain many nuggets of truth, but also a healthy helping of revisionism. Some of the errors in fact or time may be because of Jim's failing mind or impaired memory, while some of them might be Jim's attempt to remember negative events differently so as to paint things in a more favorable light. Some may be outright alibis or lies. The letters cover many topics, including Jim's version of the Northfield Bank robbery, his participation in the Roscoe Gun Battle (which differs slightly from Wilbur's earlier account), Jim's dreams for a positive future, his love of Cora Lee McNeil, the controversy about reporter Alix Muller, his suicide, and more. One element of the documents that caught my eye and answered a question that has puzzled Younger historians and those interested in their history for decades: Upon parole, why were Cole and Jim Younger forbidden to marry? That was an unusual restriction and Jim's requests to alter this requirement were repeatedly denied without given cause. I was astonished to find the answer to this perplexing turn of events.

Along with Jim's letters are letters and documents from Ms. Deane that tell the story from the memories of her mother, Cora Lee. Jim's story is further made flesh from Cora Lee's accounts.* A rare look into the life of such a historic figure is a splendid treat. All in all, these unique documents have at last given us insight into Jim Younger's life as well as allowed us at last to hear Jim's story in his own words.

---

* Unfortunately, a photograph of Cora Lee McNeil has proven impossible for me to find.

CHAPTER 1

Unfulfilled Love

IN 1877, THE JAMES-YOUNGER GANG COMMITTED ARGUABLY THE
most famous bank robbery in American history. The place was
Northfield, Minnesota. The details of that robbery—who was inside
the bank, the motive of the outlaws, who shot the cashier—continue
to be debated to this day. What is clearly historical fact is that the
three Younger brothers who participated—Cole, Jim, and Bob—
were sentenced to Stillwater Penitentiary in Minnesota for twenty-
five years to life. Bob Younger would die there in 1889 at the age of
thirty-five, the victim of consumption. A massive effort by noted
politicians and respectable men and women to request that parole
be granted to the Youngers, so that Bob might return home to Missouri to die, proved to be in vain. Cole and Jim would again apply
for parole after serving twenty-five years; the usual time those sentenced the same would serve before being released. Their prospects
looked good; the three Youngers were exemplary inmates. They held
responsible jobs in the prison, never got into trouble, got along with
Stillwater's administration, and even once during a fire were given
weapons to guard the other inmates against the possibility of escape.
One might say that the Youngers simply accepted that they were
guilty of the robbery and resigned themselves to the twenty-five
years behind bars that had been their decree. However, when other

prisoners who had committed greater crimes began to be released, the Youngers, and those who had been attempting for years to get them set free, were perplexed. The appeal of Cole and Jim fell on the deaf ears of Governor William R. Merriam, who arbitrarily decided that he was not going to release the Youngers under any circumstances. Governor Merriam didn't care that it was the "usual" practice to release prisoners after they served ten years. He didn't care that the two brothers had done all they could to repent, get along well at Stillwater and learn acceptable trades. He didn't care that important and respected men from both Missouri and Minnesota wrote letters and made personal appeals to see that the Youngers were set free. Merriam held a secret: his father had been one of their victims, humiliated at the hand of one of the outlaws—likely Jesse James—who robbed a train on which he was a passenger at Gad's Hill Missouri in 1874. That was enough for Governor Merriam. He preferred that Cole and Jim Younger rot in jail.

There's no denying that Merriam was angry, unforgiving, and vengeful. Yet new information from years past suggests that there was more to the story. That quite possibly the only reason the Youngers were released at all was because of the interference and involvement of a Minnesota judge who had his own agenda that had nothing to do with the honorable release of two men who had paid their debt to society. The judge's purpose was to manipulate the laws of Minnesota to serve his own best interest.

Yet in order to understand all this, we must know more about the brothers' history, Jim's in particular. The story may have played out for Jim Younger in Minnesota, but it began in Missouri.

The marriage of Jim's parents, Henry Washington Younger from Crab Orchard, Kentucky, and Bursheba Leigh Fristoe from McMinnville, Tennessee, was a blending of prestige and pioneer spirit. Henry's family had relocated to Missouri seeking new opportunities, and Henry eventually became the owner of hundreds of acres of land, a livery, and a general goods store. He was active in local politics and community affairs both in Jackson County and Cass County. Bursheba was the daughter of Judge Richard Marshall Fristoe, who served on the bench in Jackson County, Missouri. After Henry and Bursheba married in 1830, the couple wasted no time in starting a family and laying down roots deep into the soil of Western Missouri. They would enjoy fourteen children: Laura Helen ("Laura"), Isabelle Frances ("Belle"), Martha Anne ("Anne"), Charles Richard ("Dick"), Mary Josephine ("Josie"), Caroline, Thomas Coleman ("Cole"), Sarah Ann ("Sally"), James Hardin ("Jim"), Alphae, John Harrison, Emily J. ("Emma"), Robert Ewing ("Bob"), and Henrietta ("Retta").

Their third son, Jim Younger, was a quiet young man. Extremely intelligent, Jim never was as popular as his older brothers Dick and Cole, choosing to read books rather than socialize or become involved with politics or community issues. Education was very important to the Younger family. Dick attended college and in those early years, their cousin Stephen Carter Ragan privately taught Cole, Jim, and the Younger daughters.

After the trauma visited upon his family during the Border War and the War between the States, Jim became even more introspective. The murder of Henry Younger at the hands of militia officer Irvin Walley was devastating to Jim and his family. Jim had been at the party where Walley and his brother Cole came into conflict, and it was the altercation between Cole and Walley that eventually resulted in the murder of Cole and Jim's father in retribution. It had been Jim who had been "in charge" of the family while Henry was on his ill-fated trip to purchase goods for his dry goods store, only to be killed on his way home. Family meant everything to Jim. The

3

ever-faithful young man thought he should join Quantrill's group of Confederate Irregulars to seek vengeance for all that Irvin Walley had taken from his family, but Cole convinced Jim to stay at home to watch over their mother and younger brothers, John and Bob. It was Jim who hid in the field lest he be arrested when the Union Army ordered his mother Bursheba to take what few possessions she could and then burn the family home to the ground. Jim was overseeing the safety of his family when over 100 young women, including his sisters Josie, Caroline, and Sally, were taken to a makeshift jail by Union soldiers—a jail that would collapse, killing several and injuring dozens. By the end of those turbulent war years, Jim Younger suffered suffocating guilt from not being able to keep his family safe. He would devote the rest of his life to the wellbeing of his family, no matter the personal cost.

"Jim Younger maintained always the deep rooted mystery of their father's murder, the robbery and the persecution of the family, stemmed from the murder itself," writes Deedee Deane. "Colonel Younger made no secret of the fact that he was a Union man. He owned no slaves. All the Negros working for him were on salary. The older ones remained because it was the only home they knew, and being human, the problem of putting down cold in new places was unthinkable to them."

After eventually joining the guerillas and his ultimate release from Alton Prison as a former Prisoner of War, Jim helped his family however he could, but he had become even more of a loner. He worked the cattle enterprise with his brothers and nurtured his lifelong love of horses. He continued to read voraciously and spent long hours in deep thought. Although he would later deny it, Jim was guilted into joining his brothers and the James boys when they committed a train robbery near Adair, Iowa, in 1873. The overturning of the train and the death of the engineer convinced Jim that he didn't have the desire or the stomach for such recklessness. He chose to sit out the rest of the robberies, save one. He dreamed not of revenge but of someday owning and directing a horse breeding business. His dreams didn't end there after Cora Lee McNeil came into his life.

It is no secret that Jim's romance with Cora Lee was important to him. Yet the depth of their relationship and its ultimate position in Jim's life—and his suicide at the age of fifty-four—have never really been revealed. Jim sought to keep his feelings for Cora Lee private and his later life was tied to the deception of a certain Ms. Alix Muller. Ms. Muller apparently lied her way into history claiming to be at the most, Jim's common-law wife, at the least his fiancé. In fact, she was likely neither. Ms. Muller declared the reason for Jim's suicide was because he was forbidden to marry and his heartbreak at not being able to make Alix Muller his wife was more than he could bear. The letters he wrote the night he died made this theory feasible. But it was not the whole truth. The letters Jim wrote to Cora McNeil seem to substantiate that.

So much of Jim's personal history has been shrouded in mystery or folklore. Examining Deedee's letters and narratives and Jim Younger's letters to her mother finally shine a light on the complexity that was Jim's life. The letters that Deedee wrote to Wilbur Zink and the material she shared with him are dated throughout the years of 1968 and 1969. They begin with an explanation of why Deedee had chosen to reveal them at that time.

"The years before our mother Cora Lee McNeil Bennett passed away in 1942, she and I had been sorting, arranging in reference, indexing for filing, the huge mass of data, consisting of letters, pictures, clippings and mementos she had accumulated during the years she worked for the release of Cole and Jim Younger from Stillwater prison in Minnesota," Deedee wrote. "It had been her intent, after many years of silence, to at last disclose the truth concerning James Younger's suicide. In so doing, she would also be revealing the identity of the woman Jim Younger ever loved.

"After Mama 'went into another room,' it became necessary for me to store my household goods and accept a splendid out of state position. In packing the Younger material, I came across a large package of letters I had not previously seen in the still unsorted matter.

"The letters were between two pieces of cardboard, tied with a faded bit of lavender ribbon. Across one piece of cardboard Mama had written, 'From a Valiant Soul who has passed Beyond. Please burn after I am gone.'

"As I read the words, one envelope slipped from the packet almost as though someone had predetermined that one letter be read before destroying the evidence, proving the singleness of Jim Younger's love for 'M.S.R. Corona, Cora Lee.'

"I had made no effort to untie the ribbon, had no thought to do so. I am positive I was not careless in the handling of the bundle. As I picked it up, I was startled to see the envelope was addressed to my mother, 'Mrs. George M. Bennett, Deadwood, South Dakota, 52 Taylor Avenue' in Jim Younger's large, heavy writing. The postmark read, 'Mailed on train, St. Paul, Minn, 8:00 p.m. Special Delivery, October 18th 1902.'

"On the back was the receiving postmark, 'Deadwood South Dakota, 1:00 p.m. October 20th 1902.' There was no return address on the envelope that I held, forty years after it had been mailed.

"In our home mail was not read or opened by anyone other than to whom addressed unless requested to do so. That was a cardinal rule, strictly adhered to. Believing strongly in the Occult (not Spiritualism) as I did then and still do, I was strangely impressed that somehow from out of the unknown it was intended as a message to me, not to be ignored. I was to read that particular letter before I did as Mama had requested, 'please burn.'

"I may have been wrong. I had been shown many of Jim's sketches across the top of his letters, yet was never told to read the personal letter which followed. At the time, the sketches had no meaning for me, only as pen and ink work. I, of course, asked no questions. Mama gave no explanation, as to 'Corona' and 'The Old Fool.'

"Yes, I read the letter and have no regrets. It was so beautiful, an expression of the tremendous love that lay between my mother and Jim Younger. A love deep-rooted and steadfast, defying circumstances beyond their ability to overcome.

"Before destroying the letters, as Mama requested, I did copy excerpts that held a strange fascination for me."

Deedee wrote to Wilbur Zink why she was, at the late date of 1968, finally releasing Cora Lee's letters and recollections. Cora Lee had dictated her remembrances of Jim to Deedee and long ago had written a fictional account of their relationship in a book she titled *Missoura*.

"Mizzoura was primarily to be the story of Cole and Jim Younger, their lives in a 'throwback' of pre-Civil War days or as writers of today express it, 'Antebellum'," Deedee wrote. "Thru young manhood, their war experiences pre and during, then

7

past. It was to include the true love stories of both in the hope such a book could offset the trash that had been presented by so many writers as having been personally dictated by the Youngers, when in reality no one writer ever met either Cole or Jim during their entire imprisonment except Cora Lee."

Deedee writes of the trials and tribulations of Cora Lee's desire to tell her story:

"Jim's only reason for not consenting to take his place in the story, he feared adverse publicity for Cora Lee. However she stoutly maintained she was not ashamed of what had been between them. All their relatives and friends were aware of their love. Even if Jim did not want her to take the risk.

"Cole was against it also. You will doubtless see his motive, if you have read Mizzoura and realized it is almost Cole's love story. Judge Bennett's attitude was a big factor in Jim's decision. Nether Cole or the Judge fooled Jim Younger one little bit.

"You have wondered why in the forty years between the tragic and needless death (1902) of Jim Younger and my mother 'going into another room' (1942) she did nothing with the vast amount of material she had regarding Jim's reluctant participation in the Northfield Affair.

"The first twenty-three years, my stepfather Judge George M. Bennett, was the stumbling block. . . . Years after the Judge's death, the depression having hit us hard, Mama decided she would break her silence, try to do something with her material. Thru Lee Shippey of the Los Angeles Times, she contacted an agent in Hollywood, a

Mrs. Alvard, who had connections with Warner Bros. and in good faith she took Mizzoura to the studio.

"This was in the fall of 1941. In Jan. of 1942 Warners, thru Mrs. Alvard, offered $5000.00 for all rights to Mizzoura, all material, letters, pictures pertaining to the Youngers, [her to] sign a statement that [she] had not reserved anything. Mama had written Mrs. Alvard that I held her Power of Attorney, as she was not well enough to attend to negotiations.

"Of course Mama refused this offer. I requested the return of the book. Warners ignored my letter.

"Mama passed away April 20th, 1942. My Power of Attorney was no longer valid. Not being financially able to fight Warner Bros. by myself, I went to an old friend, Ray Nimmo, who at the time was Prosecuting Attorney for Los Angeles. He did not want to write a letter. He phoned— told some 'top brass' to return the book immediately or else. When I returned home to Temple City, the studio representative was waiting with the book.

"Months later, Warners produced 'Bad Men of Missouri' but in no way did they infringe on Mizzoura. They were fully aware the copy write had expired.

"The Judge, as Mama's attorney, took over the management of the book's publication. I believe I told you he knew as much about it as I do about harpooning a whale, which is absolutely nil. He gave away the first 600 copies to come off the press. You will see by now the Judge was not on my list of people I was fond of or most liked to be with.

"Without Mama's knowledge or consent, he had obtained the copy write in his daughter's name of 'Gorgas.' She was Georgia Mae (Mrs. C.O. Gorgas). The printer made it E.M.

"When the 26 years copy write was about to expire, the copy write office in Washington D.C. said that unless Mrs. Gorgas transferred the copy write to Mama before the expiration date, she (Mama) could not renew it, even tho she was the author. (Her handwriting would prove that.) Mrs. G refused.

"As an adult, I often expressed my personal opinion of the Judge and his daughter, as I did in 1939 when I was doing her dictation. Mama, gentle soul that she was, merely said, 'My Robin Song, they are both dead. They cannot give their rebuttal.' (That was a word I tossed about airily while reading Blackstone and crammed six years into four—succeeding in ruining my eyesight.)

"I had stored my seven rooms of furnishing with a supposedly good friend and distant relative at her insistence 'to save storage payment, no charge, leave them as long as you like, take them when you wish.'

"My doctor suggested a change. I was restless and terribly lonely. I had a good position offered me in Seattle and was away a year.

"Returning to California, I built a home. When I was ready for my things, my dear old friend (?) said they were no longer mine. From time to time I had sent money for the storage but the only other person who knew the storage arrangements was dead. I lost everything.

"Lucky for me, I had left a box with my oldest brother Lloyd Earl Deming that contained the letter of Cole re the Younger-Daniels-Lull affair and the notes I had compiled that I expect to send to you. As you know, I sold Cora's letter to Mr. Hamilton. Also the pictures of Cole-Jim-Bob and the one taken with their sister Rhetta Rawlins of

Dallas. I did not even get Jim's drawings, which I will tell you of later on, or Jim's last letter before he died.

"Jim always used a stub pen. His writing was heavy, somewhat large but legible. His personal letters to Corona were always in sketches, two and one half inches in height, sometimes three inches, depending on the subject of his sketch, which reached across the top of a page, left to right.

"On the left, 'Corona.' The features were those of Mother as she looked in 1876, but with a Gainsborough setting, plumed hat, beautiful lace fichu around the neck and shoulders.

"To the right in profile was 'The Old Fool' in the usual garb of a Court Jester. The face was that of a gargoyle, grotesquely distorted, like a mask worn by dramatic actors in olden times. The features never changed in either one of the representations, only the scenes between were different. There was no interpretation in words, the sketch alone conveyed 'The Old Fool's' message to his 'Corona MSR.' To Jim Younger my mother was Corona, as well as Cora Lee. Corona was his crown and M.S.R. My Soul's Reward.

"There were high, steep jagged mountains, the tops veiled in clouds or mists. Snowcapped in others, deep in white silence, chasms deep and wild, with a turbulent stream racing over and around the huge boulders. Terrific thunderstorms, flashes of lightning, gales bending and twisting the trees.

"Others pictured wooded glens, placid meandering rills. An old rut filled road fading over a distant hill. Tree studded mountains with a lake in the valley, a lone eagle soaring high overhead. Tall grasses across endless miles of prairie, wild, lonely. In all the years they were sent to Corona, not one showed the faintest similarity or connection with any other sketch.

"The figure on the left was always Corona. The one on the right 'The Old Fool Jim Younger', Stillwater, Minn. Prison and the date.'

"For years my one desire has been, or may I amend that and say it has been an obsession, that the work my mother did for the Youngers be made known and of Jim's part in her life.

"Outside of the knowledge of Jim's deep love and his appreciation of her efforts in the Youngers' behalf—thwarted by my step-father of her rightful share of publicity in their eventual release on parole, to say nothing of the years of happiness Jim and his Cora Lee might have had together, not one cent did she derive from her years of work. Cole it was who gained the most—the full pardon Jim prayed for and the opportunity to return to Missouri and a normal life . . .

"I have told you this bit of sordid history long since buried like Deva, so that you may know the answer of 'why' after these sixty-two years of silence, I am so determined to give my Mother her just credit, posthumous tho it may be.

"All parties have entered Jim's Nirvana. I feel I am free to divulge and rectify the injustice done to two people who had a great influence in the shaping of my character and life, my devoted mother whom I loved with all my heart, almost I worshiped her, and Jim Younger, who as Mama said was a 'Valiant Soul.'"

CHAPTER 2
A State in Turmoil

THROUGH THE LETTERS RECEIVED BY CORA LEE O'NEIL FROM Jim Younger during his time in prison and the year after his release, a poignant and very different story emerges from the one we know so well. The purpose behind the conditions for the release of James Younger, after serving his time in a most favorable and respectful manner, would be revealed at last. Yet to truly understand those conditions and their effect on Jim, we need to go back to the roots of Jim's story, told through those letters . . .

Stillwater, Minnesota
Oct 18, 1898
"The first time I saw you, my Cora Lee, was in the late fall of 1865,"wrote Jim in a letter to Cora Lee McNeil. "I had been taken prisoner after the battle in Kentucky in which Quantrill was killed. That was my first and last taste and in fact my only taste of actual civil warfare.

"I never knew Quantrill; I was not in his company. I never rode with him in any of his raids, never spoke to him in my life and only knew him by sight. Doubtless to him I was just another Missouri country boy."

While Jim freely offers names and dates to Cora Lee in his letters, there is a certain amount of revisionist storytelling as well. Why Jim would deceive the woman he loved is not easily understood. Did he simply not want to own up to some of the questionable decisions he had made? Or had he simply, in his own sensitive and romantic mind, chosen to either forget them or put them squarely in his past, to be forgotten so that he could pave the way to a better future? Because Jim did indeed know William Clarke Quantrill, the leader of the Missouri guerrillas, under whom his brother Cole had served.

Jim likely did not know Quantrill well, and it is possible that Quantrill knew Jim only by sight and name. Jim watched his familiar family life implode due to the oppression of the Union Army and State Militia as they sought to immobilize Quantrill, the Confederate forces and of special concern to Jim, their faithful soldier Cole Younger. After so much time dealing with the various dire circumstances of the effect the war had on his family, Jim had realized that the war needed to come to an end. He felt that he had not done enough toward this end and joined with Quantrill's men in the spring of 1864 at the age of sixteen. Jim was useful to Quantrill as a scout, since he knew the area so well and could travel a little more freely than others already known to be Quantrill's men. Jim would serve with the guerrillas for a year. Whether he was involved in any skirmishes or battles during that time, we don't know.

Jim was with Quantrill when the leader made his way to Kentucky with a small band of men in May 1865. On May 10, the guerrillas stopped for the night near Louisville at the farm of a Southern sympathizer named Jeremiah Wakefield. Their tracks having been discovered by Union Captain Edwin Terrill as he and his men passed the barn, Quantrill and his men were at last left vulnerable. As they slept in Wakefield's barn, Terrill and his men quietly and quickly advanced on the irregulars in a cacophony of gunfire. When the smoke cleared, Quantrill lay unconscious and nine of his men were taken prisoners. Quantrill was taken to the military hospital in Louisville, where he died several days later.

Guerilla John McCorkle later wrote:

And they captured Dick Glasscock, Jim Younger, Bill Gaugh, Vess Aker, Jack Graham, Dick Burns, George Robinson, Tom Evans and Andy McGuire. These last nine named were taken to Lexington and placed in jails and on three different occasions were taken out into the jail yard to be hung, but each time the boys would come out of the jail cheering for Jeff Davis and daring them to hang them, telling them their deaths would be avenged.

Jim and the other men were eventually taken to the federal prison at Alton, Illinois, where they remained until months after the end of the war. (Cole was laying low at their Uncle Coleman Younger's ranch in Northern California, ostensibly to raise money for the Confederacy.) When Jim was finally released to return home, it was with the stipulation that he swear the Oath of Loyalty. Agreeing to be loyal to the very people that had caused the death of his father and the devastation of his family made him physically, mentally, and emotionally ill but he had no choice. It became one more piece of guilt that would hang over the young man's head.

"Gen. Lee surrendered in April of 1865," Jim continued. "I had been sent to the Union prison in Alton, Ill. And was not released until late fall of that year. I still had a bad shoulder wound and the prison surgeon advised me to continue medical care, as the wound was slow in healing.

"He then asked where I would locate. I told him at my home in Missouri. 'Too bad you won't be near my good friend Dr. McNeil', he remarked. 'But I will be, sir, if you refer to Dr. D.C. McNeil of Osceola, Mo.', I replied.

"It looked for a moment like he was going to hug me, then thought, better not to be too cordial, shook my hand instead saying 'Good, good. There is no better surgeon any-where that I know of. We went through the mess together. Tell him I sent you. It was he that suggested my commis-sion, Brevet Major, yet he would not accept a commission himself. Give him my best regards.'

"You will remember, my Cora Lee, I did look up your father; in so doing I found you. Did you ever wonder at the care and how often the visits that shoulder required? (Brevet Major King would have approved.)"

Dr. D. C. McNeill was one of the most popular and respected doctors in St. Clair County, Missouri. He had served as a surgeon for the Union Army during the war and then returned to his family in Osceola where he doted especially on his pretty young daughter Cora Lee.

"As the years went by we were drawn to each other by our mutual interests, good literature, poetry, the best in classical music," Jim remembered. "My hobby being horses (no pun intended), you being an experienced equestrian, our fondness for 'Equuscabella', proved to be a good excuse, if any was necessary, to explore together the miles of bridal paths that wound along the bluffs of the old Marais des Cygnes.

"A ball at the Osage Hunt Club aided by musical parties, on the moon-lit river with Cole and his fiancé, your two older brothers and their young ladies, made falling in love with each other inevitable. Your brothers George and Oscar were two of our closest friends, and are yet. Cole can never forget the offer George has made to President McKinley."

Jim mentions "Cole's fiancé" without naming the young lady. It is possible that Cole was in love with Elizabeth Brown. The story of Elizabeth and Cole is a complicated one. Nicknamed Lizzie, Elizabeth was the daughter of Robert and Mary Brown of East Tennessee. The Brown family moved to Cass County in 1842 with over forty slaves. Robert Brown became a successful landowner and constructed the first steam gristmill and sawmill in Cass County and eventually established a tannery. In 1851, the family moved into a lovely home known as Wayside Rest.

It has long been thought that Cole was romantically involved with Lizzie, many assuming that from several references he made as to her being his "sweetheart." Lizzie's family, on the other hand, claims that the two were just good friends and were never romantically involved. Since it is not uncommon for those once involved with notorious people to hide the status of their previous relationships with them, this may or may not have been the case. Yet in a letter from Lizzie's granddaughter, Mary Daniel Whitney, to historian Dr. William Settle Jr., Mrs. Whitney writes that Cole said to a friend after his pardon, "I have never forgotten Lizzie I can still remember just how she looked when I last saw her. I called her 'My Old Sweetheart' but that is as far as my attachment went. We're good friends so I want to see her, for until I do, I will not be able to realize fully that I am again home."

Cole had known Lizzie since becoming good friends with her four older brothers. Her brother Tom was one of his best friends. He visited the family home often and Lizzie would entertain by playing the piano and singing. Cole later wrote to her with fondness, "You plaid and sang ever so many pieces and we enjoyed it better than we have enjoyed the best singing in the land in later years."

Deedee Deane says that her mother and Lizzie were "chums." The history of Lizzie's youthful days gets complicated when Deedee claims that Cora Lee and Lizzie attended the same finishing school in New Orleans. Although Lizzie was a year older than Cora Lee, Deedee says they were in the same class and were roommates. Lizzie studied music and Cora Lee studied voice. Lizzie's family claims that Lizzie never attended school in New Orleans.

Robert Brown had voted against Missouri's succession and resigned as a delegate to the state's convention in 1863 rather than vote for the presented emancipation ordinance. During the war, Lizzie was sent to Independence Female College but the college was closed after the Battle of Independence. She then attended Howard Female College in Fayette and later was a student at Christian College in Columbia. While there, she met Henry Clay Daniel.

Tom Brown was injured at the Battle of Pea Ridge and died shortly after. Cole remained friends with the Brown family and later wrote to Lizzie that her family was "the family of all other's on earth that outside of Mother's I loved the best." In 1868, Lizzie married Henry Daniel. Daniel by this time was an attorney. He would later become a judge and serve as Mayor of Harrisonville, Missouri. Decades down the road, Daniel would write a strong article in favor of the Youngers' parole. Deedee further claims that Cora Lee said that Lizzie's father liked Cole very much and approved of her relationship with Cole until the Northfield incident. That affair made him "very bitter," and he forbade

Lizzie any correspondence with Cole. Why Lizzie would be under the thumb of her father's direction up to that time in 1877 is questionable, since she was already married to Henry Daniel.

Cole corresponded with Lizzie while he was in prison and after his release and eventually reunited with her. They would remain close friends until Cole's death. Yet since he was a friend with both Lizzie and her husband, it is extremely doubtful that she was ever more than just a dear friend. Perhaps Cora Lee was protecting another local young lady by implying to her daughter that the character that was in love with the Cole Younger character in her fictional book *Mizzoura* was Lizzie Daniel.

The naming of President Mckinley is in reference to the massive parole drive to free Jim, Cole, and Bob from prison after they were sentenced for their involvement in the Northfield Bank robbery. Cora Lee's brother George McNeil was perhaps one of the men who intended to propose to the president that he would take the place of the outlaw brothers to serve out the remainder of their sentences. This was offered to demonstrate the faith and commitment to the Youngers by upstanding citizens of Missouri and Minnesota. The idea was quickly dismissed.

After the Osage Hunt Club ball, Jim and Cora Lee fell in love and discussed their desire to eventually marry. Jim first had family obligations to fulfill, and of course he would want to decide on an acceptable and monetarily profitable way to earn a living that would support Cora Lee and any children with which they might be blessed.

CHAPTER 3

Looking toward the Future

Jᴵᴹ ʟᴏᴏᴋᴇᴅ ꜰᴏʀᴡᴀʀᴅ ᴛᴏ ʜɪꜱ ꜰᴜᴛᴜʀᴇ ᴡɪᴛʜ Cᴏʀᴀ Lᴇᴇ ᴡɪᴛʜ ɢʀᴇᴀᴛ
excitement. It was something that was his and his alone, apart
from any of the problems or horrible events that had plagued his
family for so many years. But that didn't mean there were not
difficulties yet to come. At this point in his letter to Cora Lee,
Jim speaks to some of his past troubles after his return to his
nonmilitary life:

"In 1871 Cole and Bob were still in Louisiana, John was with
me in Dallas," he writes. "He was bookkeeper in a general
store, was well liked. He fell in with a crowd of older more
reckless men, drank some, never to excess but I did not
approve and told him so quite bluntly in urging him to
break away from that rough element.

"I had always been the 'big brother' that {John} and
Bob brought their troubles to (Cole leaving for the Service when they were little boys) but John just shook his
curly head, grinned and said, 'Big brother, you sound
like an old maid aunt. Just because you and Bud don't
approve of my drinking and you don't smoke, don't lecture me.'"

In another letter to Cora Lee, Jim provides a little different story:

"John's episode in '71, occurred while I was out of town," he writes. "Finishing up the taking of the ninth census of the U.S. Texas being the last of the Southern States to secede had been re-admitted to the U.S. March 30, 1870, thus completing the so-called reconstruction of the Southern States. The census enumeration had been a vast undertaking, for me at least. I was clerk and day deputy to Sheriff Nichols, my territory was large, ranches scattered, communities miles apart.

"Cole was in Florida. Bob was attending William and Mary College. John's episode occurred on January 15, the birthdate of Cole and I, born four years apart, Cole in 1844—I in 1848."

Much has been made of Bob attending William and Mary College but although Cole wanted his little brother to enroll and gave him the money to do so, it never happened. In the first place, Bob was not formally educated so his being admitted to such an esteemed institution is doubtful. Bob later said he didn't feel he fit in, which would be natural, but he likely never even reached the location of the college after Cole took him to the southeast to allow him to travel on alone to the institution. No documentation of Bob's enrollment has been found by staff at William and Mary. Shortly after Bob's trip east with Cole, Bob relocated to New Orleans, where he found work on the docks.

Jim Younger was fond of both of his younger brothers but spent more time with his brother John. He wrote Cora Lee:

Our brother John was inherently a happy-go-lucky type of person. His was a sunny disposition. He was generous to a fault. He was not the reckless devil-may-care sort Cole often called him.

As a small boy, John realized he had a quick temper, which he made every effort to control without help from anyone. Often when something went wrong, if he felt his temper rising, he would abruptly walk away to be alone until he was sure the impulse had passed. He definitely had his serious side also. Father often remarked, "That boy is the spitting image of my brother T.J." (Thomas Jefferson Younger).

John Younger never looked for trouble. If it came, he met it as best he knew how. He did not worry, his theory being the things that people worried about seldom happened anyway. It was less bother to wait and see what was going to occur and appraise the net result, thus he expressed life as he saw it.

Neither Cole, Bob or I used liquor, nor did Bob and I smoke. While we did not condone John's drinking, we did not lecture him, as he was not a compulsive drinker, he could take it or leave it. I never knew him to drink to excess, nor did he smoke.

His gentle side was his closeness and love for his family. He would not tolerate the abuse of any dumb creature. He did not care for hunting and fishing. Neither did I.

Jim continues his story about John's "episode in '71":

A few days later John had his trouble with young Russell, caused by a thoughtless prank. I was clerk and a deputy to the sheriff but was not in town that day so I am not in a position to make a positive statement.

23

The next day I suggested John go to Missouri to our sister. He was willing and with a friend, Tom McDaniels, he left Dallas.

Jim cleverly dances around the facts of this encounter. Although he claims that his brother John did not drink to excess, John in fact was hung-over on many mornings while working as a clerk at a general store owned by Zeb Orcutt. John was well liked by the proprietor of the store, who warned him to clean up his act before he had no choice but to fire the young man.

The "thoughtless prank" Jim refers to occurred when a well-lubricated John accepted a dare to shoot a pipe out of the mouth of Joe Russell, who was sweeping the floor of the bar where John and his friends were carousing. John came to his senses before causing harm to Russell, but one of his friends jokingly advised Russell to report the abuse to the sheriff, believing that Russell would not do that. But he did. Sheriff Jeremiah Brown had no recourse but to bring John in for questioning. Yet the ever-charming John was able to convince his friend Deputy Charles Nichols—who had only been on the job one day—to allow him to turn himself in come morning.

The next morning all hell broke loose. After Nichols and his friend James McMahan went out to where John was living, they found John eating his breakfast. Self-assured and brash, John asked if he could finish his meal and offered to have the two men join him. Nichols declined the offer and said that John could finish his meal but to then present himself at the general store where Nichols and McMahan would be warming themselves by the stove.

John didn't want any trouble with the law but took his time meeting up with Nichols. He and his friend Tom McDaniels stopped briefly at the saloon before crossing the street to where Nichols and McMahan waited for him. As they passed the horses they had hitched to the post in front of the saloon, John was surprised to see that a guard had been placed on his horse. John and McDaniels approached Nichols with anger, loudly complaining about Nichols, lack of faith in John that he would do the right thing. Threatened, McMahan drew his gun. John countered by immediately drawing his gun in response and gunfire was exchanged. McMahon was killed instantly, at which point Nichols drew his gun and shot and wounded John. McDaniels then fired at Nichols, who would die four days later as the first lawman to be killed in Dallas County.

Jim tells a very different story, never mentioning anyone getting killed:

"The evening of January 15, 1971—upon my return to town, several people told me of the incident, all varied, of course," writes Jim. "Odd how no two people see alike. Makes no difference whether they are witness to, or repeat hearsay, everyone has to embellish the affair to their own liking. Nichols had gone home to supper so I did not hear his story. McMahan, the night deputy, had been home asleep when the fracas took place, so knew nothing, said it was a lot of hoopla, so why bother. He had no idea what, if anything, Nichols was going to do about the affair that night.

"As we ate supper, John related the same story I had been told by Zeb Orcutt, owner of the store where John worked, as to what had happened. During the dinner hour, John and a number of his so-called friends had indulged in some rough antics and on a dare John had shot a corncob pipe out of Joe Russell's mouth.

"John admitted to me it was a foolish thing to do and he should have showed better sense, agreed it could have resulted in grave repercussions other than just sore lips for Joe for a few days.

"The next morning before breakfast, Nichols and McMahan rode up. Aunt Suze went to the door and in no uncertain voice said, 'Y'all climb down offen dem cabs. Git in here, does yo' crave talk. Mah Boys ain't lettin' vittles git cold listen' at yo' gab, so get sat an lick in.' Nichols winked at me, saying 'How did she know that was what we hoped would happen?' Aunt Suze fairly smarted, 'Ain't seen the he-male that wasn't always hankerin' fo' food from de cradle to de grave.'"

Aunt Suze was a former slave who had lived with the Younger family her entire life. She was as an aunt for the boys and their sisters, helping them in their various trials while growing up, relocating to Texas with their mother, whom she tended with love, and eventually staying with their sister Retta in Texas. (Suze eventually returned to live in Missouri.)

"As we ate, John told Nichols what had happened," Jim continues. "He did not mention the dare, involving no one, admitting it was a foolish thing to do as it could have turned out to be more serious. There was no mention made of a warrant for John's arrest, Nichols merely asking John to come to the office with me later for a further talk. John agreed and both men left. A few minutes later, John and I saddled up and rode into town. On the way, one of John's cronies joined us—Tom McDaniels, whom I considered a rowdy and told John so on numerous occasions.

"Arriving at the office, I left my mount ground hitched as always, at the tie rack beside Nichols and McMahan's. Mc would be off duty when I reported in.

"John and Tom turned in at the saloon tie rack across the street. I went into the office. I was surprised to see Joe Russell and his older brother Bill standing a little beyond the end of Nichols' desk. Nichols was seated in his swivel chair. Mc stood back and a little to Nichols' left. I spoke to Joe and Bill. They merely nodded.

"I walked to the office window where I could see John and Tom as they left the saloon. They were not over five minutes, came out hurriedly. I saw them stop and look at their mounts, then John came on the run across the street, banged through the open door, up to Nichols' desk. Leaning over toward Nichols, he demanded quietly (I knew the tone, he was angry.) 'Why did you set a guard by my horse while I was in the saloon?'

"John showed plainly he had not taken a drink so I did not interfere but turned again to look across the street. Nichols was a heavy drinker but I never knew him to lose his head. Turning he looked through the open door, saying, 'Son, I did not order a guard. I knew you would come in when Jim did. You said you would and your word was good enough for me.' Again he turned to look across the street. From where he sat, he could only see the tails of the horses so he repeated 'and I see no one.'

"I moved closer to the window, then I saw someone was standing at the horses' head between the tie racks and the boardwalk, but could not tell who it was. Before I could tell Nichols there was a man there with the horses, Tom yelled, 'That's a lie. We both saw him. He's there now.'

"John straightened up from Nichols desk, turned toward Tom as he was yelling in time to see Tom draw his .44 and aim at Nichols. John threw himself sideways; his right shoulder pushed Tom off balance as he fired. Missing Nichols, the bullet went through the cloth of McMahan's coat at his right shoulder, not touching him otherwise.

"John's momentum carried him toward Bill Russell, on my right. Joe stood just at Bill's right, then Mc a bit farther along and in front of Joe, at Nichols' left.

"Bill drew his .45, fired at John, hitting his left arm above the elbow. I jumped Bill, knocked him down and before he could get up, handcuffed him. He had dropped his .45 and it slid under a chair. As I dragged him to his feet, Mc handcuffed Joe, who had taken no part I the proceedings. Nichols was shaken up considerably. We then saw John, on my horse, was headed on the road east. Tom had raced across to his mount and rode west. The man who had stood with the horses, I learned later, ran through the saloon and out the back door when the shooting started. The last we heard from Tom's folks, he was in western New Mexico Territory, still headed west.

"Nichols and I questioned the Russells. Joe said he had no ill feelings toward John. He also admitted he and Bill had been drinking with the crowd so took the 'incident' as it was intended and he knew nothing of the horse guard. Bill had not mentioned it nor the fact that he, Bill, had tried to swear out a warrant for John. Nichols and I believed him.

"It was then I learned Bill had tried to swear out a warrant. He was out to get John and had told Nichols a lot of lies about *John*, which surprised Nichols. Knowing John, he had decided to hear John's side of the story before issuing a warrant.

"Bill refused to answer any more questions but did say some nasty things about John. He admitted he was afraid

Nichols would not arrest John and had asked a friend to watch John's horse in case John tried to leave. He refused to name the friend. Nichols said, 'Lock him up for attempted murder.'

"Bill Russell served thirty days for disturbing the peace. As John had not even drawn his gun and left town without disclosing the extent of his injuries, I could not prefer charges. Bill Russell was a very remorseful young man the day I unlocked his cell. I offered him my hand. He took it in a strong grip. We both grinned. Both knew he had grown up in those thirty days. I told him so—adding hope John had. Bill surprised me by saying, 'He has but he didn't have to go as far as I did.'

"The affair was never mentioned again as Nichols said, 'The whole thing started with a lot of horsing around by a bunch of merry-andrew clowns, so let it lay.' I agreed fully."

In his autobiography, Cole doesn't whitewash the event and clearly states the events as they happened, with Nichols being shot by McDaniels and McMahan being shot by John. He even goes so far to say: "I was in Louisiana at the time, but on my return several attorneys offered to defend John, if he would return for trial."

Odd that in one letter, Jim says he strongly advised John to leave the area and in another he says John lit out on his own.

Jim takes up the story:

I did not hear from John until about the first of February. I worried, of course, knowing he had little money with him and was wounded. How badly I had no idea. My worry was needless. He made Little Rock, Arkansas late one cold stormy afternoon. Rode into a livery stable and feed yard. He was cold and hungry, thought he might sleep in the loft.

He was surprised to find the owner was Wade Blayne, who had managed Father's livery and feed yard in Harrisonville, Missouri. Came the war, Wade joined J.E.B. Stuart, was at Brandy Station in '63 and lost a leg at Yellow Tavern in '64 where Stuart was mortally wounded.

With a disabled discharge from General Lee, {Blayne} returned to Missouri to find his native state overrun with carpetbaggers. He married Allie and they moved to Arkansas and settled. They wanted no part in Missouri's upheaval.

John told Wade frankly why he left Dallas. Showed Wade his arm, which aside from being painful was not too serious. He had purchased a tin of axel grease and ten cents worth of white muslin for bandages of sorts. He kept the wound from worsening. Wade insisted on cleaning it up and medicating it properly as John talked. [John] said he needed work. He had spent his last half dollar for my Morgan's morning feed. Wade assured him it was lucky for both he and John that he had arrived when he did. Only that morning his night hostler, also from Missouri, had argued with a fractious Missouri mule. He should have known better. The mule won the debate. Pete Ives would be out of circulation, Doc said, about six weeks.

There was a cot in the office. John could snatch forty winks if he felt the need. There was very few customers after midnight. Wade's wife Allie had a restaurant across the street. John's salary would include the Morgan's keep. Wade wrote me all this, as he said to ease my mind, "that is if you still have one of those necessary things" and as a PS Allie wrote, "Don't worry. The boy is doing fine and is a big help to me." There was not a lazy bone *in* our brother John's body. He was a firm believer in work, any kind, as a cure-all for nearly every ill and lots of it.

John wrote he helped Allie during the rush hours for his meals. She insisted he sleep in their spare bedroom when he was not helping her at mealtime. He said I was to hold his four hundred dollars I had banked for him but if Zeb Orcutt would give me his week's pay he could buy some badly needed shirts, underwear, socks, and shoes. I read the letter to Zeb. That worthy friend added the Christmas bonus "I never got around to giving him." He said sheepishly, "You know Jim," he went on to say, "I was sorry to lose that boy. He could sell anything to anybody. Made no difference whether they wanted it or not, they bought it on John's say so. Take Sada Bruster, weighed in at 210 pounds, always said six yards of calico was all she needed to make a dress. John said one time, 'Sada Bruster, suppose you got hooked up on a barbwire sometime, what do you use for a patch?' Sada looked worried for a minute then said, 'Make it eight.' Nobody ever dares measure less than eight yards for Sada—even with John gone. That boy could charm the birds out of their trees."

Yes, our brother John had friends, a love of life, and all it held. He remained with Wade and Allie until April 1st. He then went to Kansas City. He lost no time in finding work. This time it was in hardware, wagons, buggies, harness, and saddles. I was surprised when he got his liking for that type of business, I have never figured out.

As a boy on the farm, he always seemed to know how to help make repairs on anything. No one suggested he was in the way. He anticipated every need of whoever he was helping. With his love for horses, I would have expected him to have settled on some western horse ranch. He boarded with one of our two sisters in Kansas City.

In November of '71, our uncle "T.J." was returning to California. He and his beautiful Spanish-American wife had stopped in Kansas City from some east coast visit. Both urged John to go to California with them. Never having been further than Dallas, he had saved his money. He decided to go, as he wrote me, and see the world.

There is another time discrepancy from Jim as he wrote in another letter:

In the fall of 1872, he accompanied an uncle of ours, T.J. Younger, to Calif. T.J. was establishing a winter residence in or near Los Angeles. John remained with T.J. He held a good position in a store. He had written me often, urging me to join him, as I was the only one of the family left in Texas. I resigned in April 1873, made a trip to see you, Cora Lee, and joined him in May.

Could Jim have used this time difference as an alibi for John? On September 26, 1872, three men robbed the ticket office at the Kansas City Exposition. A bullet grazed a little girl, who was standing nearby, during the ensuing escape of the robbers. The man who took the money had apparently announced that he was Jesse James. It is highly unlikely that he was the real Jesse James. Jesse would certainly not have announced his name. The real Jesse James complicated the issue by writing to the *Kansas City Times* that a Mr. James Chiles of Independence said that the robbers were Jesse and Cole and John Younger but that was impossible. Cole, known to dislike Jesse and to be in his company only in the presence of Jesse's brother Frank, was livid that Jesse himself had brought Cole and John into the story through his letter. John had never been mentioned before at all; he rather enjoyed the notoriety established by Jesse's letter. Cole didn't like John being named for a robbery he didn't commit and realized that John's nature was going to get him into trouble eventually.

CHAPTER 4
The Bonds of Family Loyalty

REGARDLESS OF HOW IT ACTUALLY WENT DOWN, JOHN YOUNGER was now off to California. Jim continues to tell of John's experience there:

John soon became restless, idleness was not for him. Unless he could find work, he was ready to go back to his old position in Kansas City.

T.J. introduced him to an old friend of his, Phillip Ruiz, a well-known merchant, dealer in hardware, saddles and harnesses. Ruiz, a wealthy Spanish hidalgo, was in need of an Americano who could handle his growing American Comerica. As John examined the beautiful handcrafted work on the saddles, Ruiz watched him, carefully eyeing the tooling on the saddle skirts and stirrup tapadera. The crafty Ruiz was well aware John knew the value and beauty of each piece of equipment. John would be an asset to his business.

Ruiz offered John a position at what John considered a fabulous salary. The young man promptly accepted, much to T.J.'s relief and delight.

John remained with Ruiz almost a year and a half and did so well he was offered a partnership, Ruiz explaining he had no "hijo" (son) to inherit the business. In April of 1873, John wrote asking me to take a leave of absence, come to California. He felt the need of big brother Jim's advice before committing himself. Realizing the opportunity was most flattering and generous, with no financial investment on his part, the responsibility was greater than he was capable of or should assume at his age. Knowing John, I was sure there was something else that bothered him also.

The holiday season of '71 was a happy one for mother and Rhett, Cole and Bob were with us a week and there were many gay parties. But by spring, I could see Mother was restless. She missed her family. They were so scattered. I wrote the girls in Kansas City to urge her to visit them, remaining a while or making her home there permanently. Sis too needed the change.

Another time discrepancy pops up here, as Bursheba Fristoe Younger actually died on June 6, 1870.

" The girls were delighted and by fall Mother and Rhett, with Aunt Suze, were on their way," Jim continues. "Christmas of 1872 was a lonely one for me. Though I had made many friends and there was no lack of invitations, I managed to get through the winter. Nichols was in bed two months. McMahan and I carried on with two deputies. Then Mc was out for six weeks. By and large, by spring 1873, I began to feel I too needed a change. "

Again, we are faced with a very interesting upheaval in the facts. The Dallas County Sheriff's Department, as well as other official entities, clearly has Nichols and McMahan being killed in Dallas on January 15, 1871, during a confrontation in their office while they attempted to arrest a man known as John Younger. Are these statements by Jim of his association with Nichols and McMahan a continued part of his cover-up of the incident, Jim's obvious problem with the accuracy of the time of events, or was his mind playing tricks on him?

" Nichols was back, also Mc, " Jim continues. "Neither felt good but I took the proffered two weeks and loafed. On my return to the office, Nichols and his force were snowed under by rustling a range war and as Mc expressed it, 'just plain cow chasers, cussedness and cattle owners range grabbin' nesters fencin', all spell trouble.' This was in late March of '73. "

Jim had arrived in Texas in the winter of 1872. Even though he was mostly interested in horses and an eventual business concerning the breeding of such, he joined the Dallas Police Department and served as one of nine policemen under Marshall Tom Flynn. Jim wasn't able to totally escape his family's (namely Cole's) reputation, however. A robbery took place in February 1873 and Jim and fellow policeman J. J. L. Hollander were accused of being the perpetrators. It's unlikely that Jim was involved; it wasn't his nature, but rather than be arrested, Jim left Dallas. Hollander was found guilty and sentenced to five years in prison.

" A month later I received John's letter and decided on the leave of absence, as things were pretty well in hand, "

Jim continues. "Nichols accepted my badge, assuring me it would be waiting for me at any time. John would be welcome too, every one spoke highly of him and all old scores had been forgotten."

In another letter, Jim had indicated that he was working with the horses on a ranch managed by J. D. Prichard in Texas at this time. This scenario seems much more likely. It's doubtful John would have been welcomed back to Dallas to work for the sheriff (!) while he was a wanted man.

"Taking the census in 1871 north of Dallas, I made my headquarters at Gainesville, a small town then, situated on the Elm Fork of the Trinity River," Jim recalled. "The California Trail crossed at that point, a few miles south of town, still on the Elm Fork. I rode across mile upon mile of lush grass, billowing gently in the summer breeze, a veritable sea of green. I made inquiries and learned that thousands of acres lay open to public filing.

"Sitting there while Blue Boy [Jim's favorite horse] made a glutton of himself, I dreamed of you Cora Lee and of peace and quiet and could see hundreds of horses on that grass."

Regardless, Jim was soon California-bound himself.

Arriving in The Pueblo del Rio de Neustria La Reina de Los Angeles de Parciuncula, literally meaning "The River of our Lady, Queen of the Angels," named for the Virgin Mary, commonly called "Our Lady of the Angeles": or if you were American and in a hurry, just "Los Angeles."

The overland stage terminal was at the Pico House, I was told before I left Dallas, and that is where I planned to make my headquarters. However T.J. and John had practically haunted the hotel ever since I had written as to the day of my departure. They were waiting for me. T.J. hooted at the idea of my staying at the Pico House. "With that shanty up on the hill where John stays? No sir-ee. We'll manage."

The "shanty up on the hill" turned out to be a three-story affair. Six rooms each floor and quite elegant. That evening T.J. and I listened as John related Ruiz's offer. T.J. agreed with me. It was a once in a lifetime opportunity. It was also placing a heavy responsibility on young shoulders and brains. Even so, I knew if he accepted the offer, he would in time make good.

I still had the impression there was more to John's hesitancy, so I said, "Now, little brother, tell us what is really bothering you." His reaction was something to see and immediate. He grinned in relief and blurted, "As Bud would say, Oh jingle bells. I thought you would never ask me."

Senor Ruiz had four beautiful daughters. The eldest, Senorita Carmenlita Antoinette Maria, was four years John's senior and Papa had hinted she was not averse to becoming Senora Younger. John said he liked all the girls but as to marriage, he much preferred a rosy-cheeked Ozark lass of his own choosing. John further revealed Carmenlita had quite a temper along with her flashing black eyes, jealous and possessive disposition. Here I quote my little brother John: "All my life I have had to learn the hard way to control my temper. So what would happen, if married, we both exploded at the same time?"

T.J. offered his favorite quotation, "There would be Hades to pave and no tar hat. Boy, that Spanish negocio and boda isn't for you. Better dejar pronto." John's knowledge of the Spanish language was far ahead of mine at the time, but I knew enough that I was sure T.J. agreed with my idea and John's unspoken hope. "Another thing," said John rather decisively. "I would always be Papa Ruiz' son-in-law." Intimating he preferred making his own way in the world, independently.

I suggested we let the matter coast along. John could, to all appearance, be giving it serious thought. He continued to escort Carmenlita to dinners and balls, often to the Merced Theatre. Always on those occasions accompanied by a duenna. John would have been reluctant to do escort duty otherwise. Our training, by our mother, was that a chaperone was a must.

All else aside, I sensed that John was homesick. The young people in his set made him one of the crowd. We were a close-knit family. We four boys were especially close, and having eight sisters, he missed the comarada of his growing up years. He had seen all of the world he cared to. He was homesick for Old Missouri.

I earnestly tried, during the next two weeks, to fit myself into some type of employment. I did not speak Spanish fluently. Mine was a mish-mash—sufficient in Texas, but not in California. Nothing appealed to me but horses. With them I was on sure ground, but with my limited means I could not afford breeding stock such as I saw and admired on the streets of Los Angeles. I disliked the continued dry, hot weather. So I was homesick too. Admittedly, only to myself, I thought.

I was wrong. T.J. saw it and remarked, "Out with it, Jim. Let's the three of us talk it out." That did it. I outlined my long cherished dream of the Texas ranch, raising and training the type of Calvary mounts demanded by the government and that I knew the market existed and had such a ranch location in mind in Texas, northwest of Dallas.

Jim had written in a previous letter,

John and I had a long talk with T.J. I described the range grassland and my plans for the future. T.J. was in favor of the idea, suggesting we return to Mo., talk to Cole and Bob and make it a four-way concern. He would back us until we were well on our way on our own.

John surprised me with his enthusiasm, said "Count me in. I'll do my share of the work and financing." Then he gave us in detail a description of the horse HE would raise and train for his own use. T.J. and I gathered from his remarks that no one dare touch the animal but himself.

Jim continues here in the previous letter,

John was enthused, said why not make it a foursome with Bud and Bob? I said the lack of capital was the main drawback with the entire deal. Cole I knew was interested more in beef than in horses, especially a new breed in America. A recent import from Scotland, Black Angus, and another from England, White-faced Herefords. T.J. suggested writing Cole of the idea. If he was interested, T.J. would advance us a substantial sum, at low interest, long-term payment.

I wrote that night. I had told {Cole} of John's dilemma and he had agreed with me—it was not for John. It was with high hopes I explained our idea of the foursome, each helping wherever and whenever was needed.

We set August 1 as a tentative date for leaving Los Angeles. John was quite keen on going through the Black Hills, Dakota Territory, even though we had heard of the Indian unrest. I agreed, with the understanding that should someone who really knew of conditions gave us advice against it, we would heed it, to which he agreed.

Cole wired he and Bob were deeply interested. We were to keep in touch across the territory as to our Missouri arrival, where and when to meet. A letter from him a few days later cautioned as to weather conditions in a strange country, especially mountainous, that we knew nothing about.

By late July we had our schedule worked out. The big problem was transportation between Los Angeles and San Francisco, which left much to be desired. An iron horse on rails would have solved the problem nicely—we were about two years early.

CHAPTER 5

Robberies and the Roscoe
Gun Battle

*Deedee Deene shared a "historical fictional" version of
Jim and John's time traveling back to Missouri through the Dako-
tas, based on what she remembers Jim telling her. It is impossible to
know which part of her detailed account is in fact true.

Jim and John seemingly had adventures on their way back home
if we are to find any non-fictional accounting in Deedee's story. Jim
continues his account of when they arrived back in Missouri:

Arriving in Mo. late in February 1874, we learned to our
utter amazement we were accused of a train robbery with
the James brothers at Gad's Hill, January 31, 1874.

Actually we were at that time at the home of Mother's
sister in Omaha, Nbr., helped her husband in his wholesale
feed store, waiting for the weather to break so we could go
on to Kansas City. We bought a horse for John. Blue Boy
was glad to see me. We took off for Kansas City via St. Joe.

Jim is probably again off on his dates here, likely in an effort
to keep both his and John's activities hidden. John had enjoyed
the notoriety of *not* being named by Jesse James as having been a

participant in the Exposition robbery. He probably told Cole that if he was going to be accused, there was no reason he should not be involved in the next adventure of Cole and his friends. On May 27, 1873, a group of outlaws robbed the St. Genevieve Savings Bank in Missouri. This was likely John Younger's first bank robbery.

Cole didn't like the fact that Jesse and Frank, by the sheer fact that they were brothers, outnumbered him during their escapades. He likely wanted his own brothers to accompany him to the next "destination." He may have suggested as much and found that his little brother John was ready and willing. Youngest brother Bob was hesitant until John encouraged him to experience the adventure of it. Jim adamantly refused; he was not interested in criminal activities. Eventually, Jim was pressured into participating; having been told that all he needed to do was hold the horses. Jim, as always, likely didn't want to let his brothers down.

On July 21, 1873, the Chicago, Rock Island and Pacific Railroad was robbed in Adair, Iowa, the first robbery of its kind in the United States. This was the only time the four Younger brothers would participate in a robbery until that day in 1876 when they would meet their Waterloo. Jim was horrified and disgusted when engineer John Rafferty was killed as the train toppled off the tracks and the fireman, Dennis Foley, was seriously injured. Jim swore he would never be involved in another robbery.

Jim's denial of involvement in the eventual Gad's Hill robbery is likely accurate. Jim had no stomach for such an illegal activity after his participation in the robbery at Adair. But John found such rousts exciting and profitable. He and Bob accompanied Cole once again, along with the James brothers, to rob the Iron Mountain Railroad on January 31, 1864, at the Gad's Hill Station, 100 miles south of St. Louis. The "James-Younger Gang" was getting bolder. This time, Jesse James decided the news of his daring feat would be better publicized if he wrote the press release himself. He handed it to his victims, leaving a space for the amount of their booty to be filled in by the officials.

This robbery would later factor into the Youngers' denial of parole from the Stillwater Penitentiary, whether or not Jim was involved. Jesse James had an ill-advised idea. As a joke, the robbers made a couple of men who self-identified as bankers and business-men with ties to the railroads strip down to their underwear, with the only reason being to cause their humiliation. One of those men was John L. Merriam, the father of the future governor of Min-nesota. Mr. Merriam would not forget the incident. He called for the Pinkertons.

"A few days in Kansas City and we were on our way to Monagaw, hoping a letter from Cole would be there or perhaps he and Bob had planned on being there," Jim continued. "As I have already given you my version of the Chalk Level event, I will not dwell on it here, only to say it resulted in the tragic death of John and Deputy Daniels on March 17th, 1874. It was a terrific shock to our entire fam-ily. Greed for money and an insatiable desire for notoriety prompted the killing of two young men and the serious wounding of the perpetrator, all so needless."

The incident that Jim calls the "Chalk Level event" brought a ter-rific blow to the Younger family. In the second week of March 1874, Cole suggested the four brothers retreat to Hot Springs, Arkansas, to elude Pinkertons looking for them in their home area. In Hot Springs they could enjoy some leisure time. John and Bob liked the idea but Jim wasn't feeling too kindly about his brothers and their recent activities and didn't want to go. Cole finally convinced him that it would be a good bonding experience for all of them and Jim reluctantly agreed. The day of their scheduled departure, John was ill—likely with a hangover. Cole and Bob decided to go ahead, while Jim said he would stay with John, and they would join their brothers later in the week.

Cole had been right about the need to travel lest the Pinkertons come looking for them. Two men had checked into the Commercial Hotel in Osceola, Missouri, in mid-March, 1874. They posed as cattle buyers but were actually Louis Lull and James Wright, two men working for the Pinkerton Detectives who had been sent to investigate the Gad's Hill Robbery. Now they were in St. Clair County, looking for Cole Younger and any of his brothers who may have been involved in that crime. Lull had been a captain on the Chicago police force prior to accepting the Pinkerton assignment and Wright hailed from St. Louis. They brought a local man named Edwin Daniels into their ruse and pretended to attempt to locate the "Widow Sims," looking to buy her cattle.

Jim and John Younger were having lunch with their lifelong friends Theodrick and Sallie Snuffer near Roscoe, Missouri, on March 16, 1874, when they heard horses approaching the farmhouse. The two young men scrambled up a ladder to hide in the attic while Theodrick opened the door to greet two men on horseback, Lull and Daniels (although they of course didn't introduce themselves as such). Wright remained behind, several yards away. Snuffer told the men how to reach Mrs. Sims' house but became suspicious when the men rode off in the opposite direction. John was immediately alert to the fact that the men were not who they said they were and told Jim they needed to follow them to see what they were up to. Jim said he didn't want trouble but John convinced him of the threat. The two brothers retrieved their horses from Snuffer's barn and rode in the direction the alleged cattlemen had chosen.

As Lull and Daniels, now reunited with Wright, walked along discussing where they might find the Youngers, they heard fast approaching hoof falls. When Wright saw Jim and John approaching, he jumped on his horse and took off into the fields. Jim called at him to halt, but Wright ignored the order. Jim pulled his gun and shot at Wright, missing him but blowing his hat off his head (perhaps intentionally).

Lull and Daniels were ordered to drop their weapons, and Jim got off his horse to retrieve them. He admired Lull's English-made .43 caliber Trantor and thanked him for "the present." When the "cattlemen" responded to questions of who they were and why they were in the Roscoe area, Lull said they were just "rambling around." John pointed his double-barreled shotgun in their direction and asked if they were in fact detectives. They said they were not. John asked if they weren't, why then were they so heavily armed? Lull became belligerent and said they had the right. Daniels chimed in. John lowered his shotgun to Daniels' chest. With the Youngers' attention on Daniels, Lull quickly reached under his vest and retrieved a small No. 2 Smith and Wesson pistol. He wasted no time shooting John in the neck. Lull jumped on his horse and as Lull's horse lurched forward, John fired at him, hitting him in the shoulder and arm. Jim fired at Lull but somehow missed his target. Lull remained on his horse and fled down the road. By this time, Daniels was on his horse and he attempted to follow Lull. Jim quickly fired on Daniels, shooting him through the neck.

Lull continued riding through a grove of trees but was knocked off his horse by a low-hanging branch. John rode up to Lull as he lay on the ground. He fired twice, missing his target once but then hitting Lull squarely in the chest. While Jim rolled Daniels over to find that the man was dead, John began to ride back to

Jim. Swaying in his saddle, he looked at his brother then fell to the ground on the other side of a nearby fence. John Younger was dead.

As Lull, grievously wounded but alive, later lay in the nearby cabin of a lifelong friend of the Youngers they called "Aunt Hannah," doctors were called from Osceola to attend to him.

"Jim said he called Aunt Hannah and her 19 year old grandson who lived near," writes Deedee. "The boy rode John's horse to Osceola for Dr. McNeil. Jim waited at Aunt Hannah's who, with Jim's help, bound Lull's wounds. Willie (Wright) and John and Lull were carried to the cabin by Jim and the boy.

"Jim was not wounded. He waited for Grandfather, told the story, then rode off to send word to Cole, but not for safety sake nor of fear of arrest."

John's body was placed inside the cabin while Lull was placed on the porch. He was moved to the Roscoe House in Osceola later that evening, where Cora Lee's father, Dr. D. C. McNeill did what he could for the detective. Coming in from Chicago, Lull's wife and mother were escorted to his bedside by a Pinkerton agent as Lull's condition continued to deteriorate. After a few days, Lull was proclaimed dead and his body was loaded onto a Clinton-bound wagon where it would be placed on a train to carry it home to Illinois. Or so "they" said. Many believed that Louis Lull was NOT dead when he left St. Clair County but rather said to be so in order to keep the Youngers from retaliation should the detective live. When Dr. McNeill was asked about that possibility, he refused to comment anything other than "You must learn to keep the game in your lead." He never did reveal the truth of the matter. Yet in this letter, Jim only refers to the "wounding" of Captain Lull, not his death. This seems further confirmation that Lull was indeed alive when his "body" was removed from Missouri.

"Cole came from Louisiana for John's funeral," Jim claimed. "Bob did not, saying he and John had been so close as they grew up, had been through so much together as boys. He could not face up to it.

"I knew how he felt. Even with the family, Cole and me, it was not enough. I had you, Dear One, to comfort me, your love and sympathy. From that time on you have never failed me."

This is an interesting remembrance by Jim, as no mention has ever been made about John having a funeral. At the time of the shooting, Jim had an immediate concern that John's body might fall into the hands of his enemies. He quickly removed John's pistols, watch, and personal effects and asked his friend Speed McDonald, who had witnessed the gunfight, to "take care of John." Jim gave his horse to McDonald, asking that someone tell the Snuffers what had happened, and then took off after Wright atop John's horse.

John's family and friends were nervous that John's body might be dug up and desecrated were he to be buried in a cemetery. It was decided that he would indeed be buried in a local cemetery but his body would be placed at an odd angle so as to deter anyone from thinking it was buried there and the grave would remain unmarked. It wasn't until over a century later that a marker was finally placed on John Younger's grave.

If there was a funeral, which would have had to be one without John's body in attendance, there has been no note other than this statement by Jim. The fact is that Jim remained "missing" for about two weeks, no doubt seeking time to deal with his belief that he had not protected his little brother. He did not seek out Cole and Bob, who were in Hot Springs at the time. In fact, those two brothers knew nothing of John's death. While eating breakfast at their hotel one morning, Cole read an article in the newspaper about it. Cole and Bob were stunned. Cole wanted to immediately head to Missouri in search of Jim, but Bob said he would remain where he was in case Jim were to turn up in Hot Springs looking for them. Cole eventually met Jim on the road between the two places, as Jim did indeed eventually decide to meet his other two brothers.

"After the funeral we again discussed our mutual problems and hopes. We never lost sight of our dream of a double wedding, our Texas grassland range home," Jim recalled. "Building up a breed of stock that could survive a drive to wherever the nearest railhead would be located.

"Cole was keenly interested in two new breed of cattle he had read about [from] Scotland, because he said the days of the Texas Longhorns would soon be past history. He believed Durhams for both beef and dairy use and for beef, the white face red Shereford and Aberdeen Black Angus was the answer to every cattleman's dream.

"As you know, my forte was to be horses. With me it was to be more than an experiment for sport, or just an existence. It was to be a way of life, living in the wide-open wonderful world with all that I loved with me.

"I had talked with Major Blain at Fort Dodge, Kansas, the government buyer for the Calvary and had explained my theory of raising Morgans and Hambeltonians bred with a sturdy restrain that would have bottom, the endurance needed for long miles on the plains and with an easy gait for man and mount. The major beamed at me. 'You get that idea going, you have established an exclusive market for every mount you ready', he assured me. "

This conversation between Jim and Major Blain may have taken place during Jim and John's trip from Los Angeles home to Missouri. His recalling the conversation after the death of John demonstrates that he knew that life goes on and despite his great grief over the loss of his brother, he continued to want that ideal life with Cora Lee McNeil.

"Before Cole returned to Louisiana, after a talk with the girls, he and I decided it was time to come down to earth, " Jim remembered. "As yet we had never approached the two 'Papas' and faced the families, divulge our prospects and take our chances of being perhaps tarred and feathered. As it turned out, all the kith and kin were already aware of the facts (love is supposed to be blind?)

"Your Papa, Cora Lee, agreed with me fully, that if ever we were to marry, now was the time for me to work toward that day. He expressed his willingness to listen to our problems, would give us what help he could, but did ask that we wait two years. We agreed.

"A year later, Cole and I jolted out of our complacency after long hours of comparative figuring. Even if we both sold our growing businesses [Jim with his small horse venture, Cole with the cattle], combined our assets, we were still far short of our financial goal to start our venture.

"Another spring like the one just passed, we could then swing the things. I was of the opinion T.J. would still help out if needed.

"Cole had said he talked with Bob. Told him of John's enthusiasm and that he, Bob, said he would take John's place and work with us. I was delighted that at last, he like myself, realized we must reshape our lives if we were ever to regain any part of what the war had cost us, our family and so many other families, both north and south.

"In April of 1876, I wrote Cole. I had been offered a good price for my business, would sell and go to California to see if T.J.'s offer was still open. The boys sent me their share of expenses, knowing T.J. was still in California. I left June 21, riding Blue Boy to Omaha, where I boarded the U.P., leaving Blue Boy with Uncle Fred."

"Uncle Fred," mentioned several times by Jim in his letters, was likely an alias for his relative, as no one by that name seems to appear in the family genealogy.

CHAPTER 6

A Terrible Twist in the Road

ONCE AGAIN, JIM'S ACCOUNTING OF TIME AND DATES IS SUSPECT. He was greatly upset by the death of John and his own involvement in the incident that he felt his presence in the St. Clair area was a constant reminder of that unfortunate event both to him and to those he cared about. He felt it was best that he go out to California for a bit, if nothing else than to ease his apparent belief in the embarrassment of Cora Lee. It would also give him a chance to talk again to his uncles out there about his horse breeding plans. Yet when he arrived at Coleman Younger's home in Santa Clara, he felt that he and his brothers embarrassed Coleman and his family also. He thought maybe he should go elsewhere.

Cole had mentioned that the James brothers had a well-respected uncle with a large ranch in central California near Paso Robles. Drury James was also friendly with Uncle Coleman. Drury James had purchased a large piece of government land and later a half-interest in the Paso de Robles Hot Springs, where he built the Paso Robles Inn. He was also director of the Bank of San Luis Obispo and half-owner of the Eagle Stream Flouring Mill. (This causes one to wonder what Frank and Jesse James might have accomplished had they not turned to a life of outlawry.)

"Arriving in San Francisco I had a day layover so called on a cousin of Father's and T.J.," Jim continues. "It was a lucky day as cousin Oliver informed me T.J. would be in S.F. in two days on his summer trek to Mo. Ol then insisted I get my valise from the depot and remain with them till T.J. arrived.

"Cousin Oliver had married a beautiful California-Castilian senorita many years before. They had no children and questioned me as to my future plans. That I was willing to do justice to the answers, there was no doubt.

"When Carmen asked to see your picture, Cora Lee, I was shocked at my stupidity. It had never occurred to me to ask for one as we were seldom very long apart. I managed to give Carmen a fair description of your very long, brown hair with its flecks of gold, your large wide-apart brown eyes, olive complexion. She left the room for a few moments. Returning, she gave me a large, plush covered case. Upon opening it I saw a beautiful Spanish comb. 'It is for your "amour" she said. It is from Spain and very old. My love and blessings to you both.'

"T.J. arrived, we had our talk. When I told him Bob was taking John's share, he was pleased. 'Great crowin' geese', his favorite expression. 'That makes sense. 'Course the offer is still good.' [He] handed me a check drawn on a Kansas City bank."

T.J. (born Thomas Jefferson Younger) was more than just an uncle to the Younger boys, especially Jim, John, and Bob. After the murder of her husband at the hands of the Militia, Bursheba Younger was overwhelmed. She thought it would be a good idea to send her two youngest boys down to stay with her husband's brothers in St. Clair County.

There they would have something to do (working on their uncle's farm) and would have the stabilizing factor of men to keep them in line and from whom to learn. They first stayed on the farm of their Uncle Frank Younger in Appleton City. They also spent time with their uncles Littleton and T.J., in Osceola. T.J. was just two months older than Jim and only a few years older than John and Bob. He was more of a friend to his nephews. T.J. eventually would serve as a member of the Missouri State Legislature from St. Clair County. Ironically, in addition to being related to the outlaw Younger brothers, T.J. was also uncle to the infamous Dalton brothers, the sons of his sister Adeline.

" Oliver advised our making reservations next day, "remembered Jim. "'Riding the cars is still a novelty. You may have to wait several days.' He was correct in his surmise. I wrote Cole that day telling him T.J. was coming with me. "

Jim's narrative is quite confusing here. He says he was going to see T.J. in California. What he fails to mention is his time in the central California town of Paso Robles. Drury James had a 10,000-acre ranch just outside town named La Panza. Jim was put in charge of the horses and from all accounts loved his work there. He was at La Panza when the following incident took place, not in San Francisco with cousin Oliver, which he states. Perhaps the omission of being employed by Drury James and being on that ranch when this happened was an effort on Jim's part to continue to deny any previous association with Frank and Jesse James.

Other things were happening that concerned the Younger brothers. John Newman Edwards, editor of the *Kansas City Star*, had long been a champion of Jesse James, Cole, and the James-Younger Gang. He wrote numerous articles and editorials claiming that they were but victims of circumstance and should not be held accountable for the various "crimes" laid at their feet. Cole was delighted with Edwards' campaign to cast a better light on him. Jim thought Edwards was little more than a self-serving buffoon. When the James family farm was bombed by Pinkertons on January 26, 1875, resulting in the death of their eight-year-old half-brother Archie Samuel and the loss of their mother Zerelda's right arm, sympathy for the James boys began to rise from the local community. Engaging his influential friends, Edwards began to organize a legal action that would address the issue of the illegal activities of the James and Younger brothers.

In 1875, Legislator Jefferson Jones of Callaway County presented an amnesty bill to the Missouri State Legislature. It asked that "Jesse W. James, Frank James, Coleman Younger, James Younger, and others," since they had been "driven" to crime by the events of the War and its aftermath, be "relieved from all civil liability and all criminal punishment for all acts done by them since the 1st day of January, A.D. 1861."

It's anyone's guess what Jim thought about being publicly included in such a bill but he was in California and apparently put thoughts of it out of his mind. It wouldn't matter. Although the vote was fifty-eight in favor and thirty-nine against, a two-thirds margin was required to pass. The bill was defeated and no further action was attempted.

Jim had more personal things on his mind.

"The next evening Oliver brought a letter addressed to me, sent on from Los Angeles," Jim writes. "It was from Cole, asking if I were still with him [Oliver] [and to] please have me return at once. 'Robert is here' (here being in, I supposed, Monagaw). He signed it 'Cole'. No details, no explanation."

In fact, Jim received a postcard from Cole at the La Panza post office. It stated, "Come home. Bob needs you."

"Something was wrong," Jim continues. "Knowing Cole seldom had an explanation for most of his impulsive actions, I was more confused than usual at the wording of his short note. For one thing, we never used the name Robert. It was always 'Bob', that was the way he wanted it. Cole had always been 'Bud', not only to the family but to everyone else who knew him."

In all fairness, Cole may have used the name Robert to get Jim's attention as to the seriousness of the matter. Cole, however, claims to have used the name Bob.

"Two days later we were on our way east," Jim recalls. "At Omaha I suggested T.J. rest a few days with Uncle Fred, but being a salty old boy he insisted on riding with me, renting a mount from Fred when I picked up Blue Boy.

"We rested a day in St. Joe. At Kansas City I left T.J. with [T.J.'s] sister Mary, who said that Cole had been there but had returned to Monagaw. She did not mention Bob, who I presumed was in Monagaw with Cole and I, feeling hurried, did not ask."

T.J.'s older sister Mary was Mary Agatha Lee Younger, married to Lock Burden.

"Cole was anxiously waiting for me at the hotel," Jim continues. "He said Bob had been with friends in Kansas City but had promised to be home that afternoon and as much

as I wanted to see you, Cora lee, I could not for some
unknown reason do so until I satisfied myself as to Cole's
insisting I return home at once and his apparent agitation
in wanting Bob to be present at our talk.

"A little later Bob joined us in Cole's room. He was not
the quiet, boyish Bob of old as he restlessly paced the room.
Finally I said, 'One of you better tell me what this about.
I want to see Cora Lee, then I will tell you both our Texas
ranch is a reality.'

"Cole spoke then. I can give you what he said only as
I am sure I heard it. When he and Bob arrived in Kansas
City, they as usual, stopped at Mary's place for a few days.
Cole, anxious to see his sweetheart, left Bob, who wanted
to attend two dances coming up and promised to join Cole
the following week. Cole went on.

"The day Cole left, he and Bob met Jesse James on
the street. Bob had never met either Jesse or Frank James.
I have always suspected Jesse of following them, saw that
Cole left town then accidently met Bob again. However,
I have never voiced my opinion to Cole nor to Bob."

It is likely that Bob, having known Jesse for some time, had
previously arranged to meet Jesse in Kansas City, hoping to have
Cole in attendance to talk about a plan Jesse had.

"I do know Cole had avoided Jesse for two years," Jim claimed.

And we do know that Cole had joined forces with Frank
James, Tom McDaniels, and Tom Webb to rob a bank in Huntington, West Virginia, on September 1, 1875, so it may be true
that he had not seen Jesse in the time span Jim claims. However,

it is believed that later in that year, Cole and Frank reunited with Jesse in Tennessee.

"Jesse urged Bob to go with him to meet Frank, his brother, at their hotel," Jim continued. "They needed another man in a business [venture]. He was sure Bob would be interested. Bob was curious so he went with Jesse to his hotel to meet Frank, who was cordial. [He] said he knew 'Bud' very well."

Bob, at first curious, then as a means to gain money for the Missouri farm he was planning to buy, had already participated in three train robberies with various of his brothers and the James boys at Adair, Iowa, Gad's Hill, Missouri, and Muncie, Kansas.

"Jesse called Bob 'Boy' which Bob did not like but said nothing as Jesse began to talk," Jim continues. "'Boy, why don't you cut lose from your brothers and see the world. Join up with us in our biggest deal yet.' Bob then asked, 'Just what is this big deal?' 'We expect to run a big cattle and horse ranch in Texas soon but I'll listen to your deal,' he told them.

"'Chasing steers and broom tails ain't no kind of life for you. Now this deal is for quick and easy money, money stolen by Butler and Ames—carpetbaggers—from Southerners during reconstruction times. Maybe it was your Pa's,' Jesse reminded Bob."

Bob didn't like the cattle enterprise Cole had chosen for the family business. He was more committed to green grass and crops and had told Cole he preferred to farm. It's likely that the last time they met Bob had told Jesse that as well. Jesse likely did throw in a comment about the money Butler and Ames had accumulated through strong-arming hard-working Missouri families, including Bob's father Henry Washington Younger. He knew Bob and his family were livid over the way their family had been treated during the war, losing their property and wealth as they did.

"Bob asked where all this easy money was to be had for the taking," Jim continues. "Jesse got a map, saying 'Right up here in Northfield, Minnesota.' With three other friends who would be in the party, the six would have about twelve thousand dollars and 'no one knows us up there,', Jesse assured him.

"Bob asked who the other men were. Jesse named Charlie Pitts, Clell Miller and Bill Stiles. Frank would go as Mr. Woods and Jesse was to be Mr. Howard. Bob said he did not know the other three men and told Jesse he would need a few days to think it over."

Bob did, in fact, know Clell Miller and Charlie Pitts, although not well.

"Knowing Cole's dislike for him, Jesse cautioned Bob about mentioning their talk to Cole," Jim states. "Bob returned immediately to Monagaw [and] informed Cole he had changed his mind about going to Texas. There was something else he wanted to do."

Cole Younger disliked Jesse James immensely. He didn't like Jesse's ego—which matched his own—nor his brash behavior. He would be—and was—infuriated to think that Jesse had approached

his youngest brother with such a scheme. Jesse wanted to head the
gang and believed that Cole thought he owned that position. There
was no love lost between the men and Cole later believed that Jesse's
approach to Bob was a way to get back at Cole for their past differences.

"Cole insisted in knowing what he had in mind, that
brought on the change,"Jim continued. "Bob told of meeting Jesse, the plans, the amount of money and the names
of the members of the parties involved. Cole was amazed.
His first thought was of going to Kansas City and have
it out with Jesse. Being unable to reason with Bob, Cole
threatened to do bodily harm to Jesse unless Bob promised
to write Jesse it would be two weeks before he could leave.
Bob agreed. Cole was sure he could have me in Monagaw
before Bob left.

"As I listened to the bizarre plot I was amazed, shocked,
then furious. It was the only time in all of my life I had the
desire to destroy quickly, with malicious forethought and
intention, the life of a human being, an instinct I never felt
while I was in the Confederate Service. At the moment
my one choice of a victim would have been Jesse W. James.

"Bob would not be convinced that the scheme was fantastic, unwise and a risky undertaking. I showed them T.J.'s
check and there would be more as needed. I pointed out we
could all make a fresh start and a good living, honestly, as
we were raised. Then Cole went on.

"[When Cole first spoke to Bob about it, before Jim's
arrival] Cole said he thought Jesse was only bragging as
usual. He suggested to Bob he go to Kansas City, talk to
Frank and find out, if Bob would remain in the Springs until
he returned. Bob agreed but said if Jesse still was intending

to carry out his plans he was going along—regardless. That he was over twenty-one—could do as he pleased.

"Cole went on to say he left the next day for Kansas City, found Jesse and Frank at their hotel. Jesse was inclined to pretend surprise but Cole told him that he, Jesse, was in hopes that Bob would tell him (Cole) and that he was cordial while Jesse did all the talking. Outlining the plan, Jesse convinced Cole he had every intention of going ahead with the robbery and of urging 'Boy' to go with him.

"When Cole told Jesse that he was riding with Bob, Jesse became furious, had one of his well-known tantrums, violently accusing Cole of wanting to take over, have the larger part of the money and be boss.

"Cole threatened to use some sort of force to prevent Bob from taking part at all. As for the money, he would have no part of it. Frank intervened, apparently afraid Jesse would have one of his epileptic convection's, or try to draw his gun on Cole, knowing Jesse could not hope to outdraw Cole."

There is no evidence that Jesse had epilepsy. He did have a condition, possibly dystonia that made him blink his eyes rapidly especially when he was nervous or agitated. This may have been what Jim interpreted to be epilepsy.

"After Jesse calmed down, they completed their plans, Jesse insisting that the deal was all his idea," Jim continues. "He was head man and would give all the orders. Cole agreed for himself and Bob. At no time was I mentioned. Cole confirmed Jesse and Frank were to be Howard and Woods, as Bob had said.

"I was stunned, sick at heart, listening to Cole as he talked. Finally I asked by what pseudonym would the three idiot brothers Younger be masquerading under? I hoped my anger and sarcasm would get thru to both Cole and Bob but they remained silent. I knew Cole was worried and he knew I was."

Interesting that Jim refers to the *three* Younger brothers here. At this point in his narration, nothing has been said about Jim accompanying his brothers.

Thinking to impress Bob, I said to Cole "Bud, have you lost all sense of reason, hasn't Jesse James done enough to you in the past?" Now he is about to implicate you in this unbelievable affair through Bob. More to the point, he was confident Bob would tell you of the plan and in that wily James mind, he counted on you riding along to protect Bob then if something went wrong, the crafty Mr. Howard could tell the world it was all Cole Younger's scheme; that he, Mr. Howard, went along for the ride.

Jim may have been referring to the very first robbery Cole committed with the James boys, the Clay County Savings Association in Liberty, Missouri. The genesis of that robbery was indeed Jesse's idea. Yet Cole had no issue with helping to plan subsequent robberies and was in no way led down a path of outlawry by Jesse James.

"To Bob I said, 'You know we were raised in a good Christian home,' " Jim lamented. "Robbery, as you well know, isn't our way of life. It never has been, only through the false accusations instigated by the foxy Mr. Jesse James himself.

He is now quite sure of his ability to use you as a pawn to involve Bud, into something we could all spend the rest of our life regretting"

Robbery, in fact, had become a way of life for Cole. Bob, although stating that he had other prospects and life desires, had also committed three of them.

"Again I referred to our assured prospects in Texas," Jim continued. "Bob became impatient, said that took too much hard work over a long period of time. He wanted to make money now.

"I could see the fine hand of Mr. James cunningly painting the picture of quick wealth to Bob. For once, as it was with John, I could not reach the lad as he was at the moment and it hurt me deeply. I had lost him somewhere. I had failed. Turning to me suddenly and with more impatience he said, 'being a nurse maid to a Texas Longhorn is something I have no mind to do.' Then he stormed out of the room."

For someone who claims to have never met Jesse James, Jim seems to know a lot about him personally. Jim's dislike of Jesse began during the Gad's Hill robbery—the only robbery Jim had participated in—when he was put off by Jesse's carelessness and lack of compassion for the man who had been killed. No doubt Cole, with his ever-growing hostility toward Jesse, also filled Jim's ears with unfavorable depictions of his comrade Jesse James.

"Cole spoke first," Jim recalled. "'There it is, Jim. Where do we go from here?' I had no answer. My little world was shattered. It had taken me ten long years to rebuild it after the War to where I could see it was near completion. One little insignificant human, whom I did not even know, had with one nudge effaced it with his greed for revenge, his desire to hurt one whom he knew was a better man than he could ever hope to be.

"With all of Cole's distrust and dislike of Jesse, he said as Bob reentered the room, he would side with Bob, if we could not change his mind. Coming to me, Bob put a hand on my shoulder saying, 'Damie', his name for me when he was little, 'I hurt you. I am sorry.' I then asked if he still intended to go in the face of all our talk. He simply said, 'Yes.' That did it. I gave up the struggle, told him Cole and I were both riding, though not for the money, if the money could be taken. That if he or anyone else got out of line, I would not be responsible for what I would do. That included Mr. Howard and Mr. Woods. No innocent person was to be hurt in any way.

"Then, my Cora Lee, I saddled Blue Boy and rode in to see you. The years have not lessened or dimmed this memory of my sadness as I rode nor the moment we met. As you ran across the veranda toward me, the last rays of the setting sun caught the gold flecks in your hair and for one fleeting moment I visualized the comb in your hair, against your braids.

"One of the few things I did well that evening was to hide my heartache from you while presenting you the comb and telling you its history. It was to have been a birthday gift. It could be that standing behind you as you insisted I place it in your hair, you were unsure of my mental state, for I did have the gumption to ask for your picture, showing the comb.

"That picture has been a part of me nearly half my lifetime. Twenty-five years I have carried it by day, at night. It was within reach on my table.

"My excuse for not waiting until your birthday Oct. 18th, was our Texas deal was off and we three, Cole, Bob and I, were considering another deal in Minnesota, leaving in a few days and probably not returning until sometime in November."

Why Jim believed the Texas deal was off instead of postponed is notable. Perhaps he thought that he and his brothers would not be worthy to accept their uncle's goodwill after participating in a robbery. Jim had a lot of pride and this decision would have caused him to think ill of himself and would certainly affect his relationship with the extended members of his family. That he would make such a commitment to Bob, on such short notice, demonstrates his deep love and concern for his little brother. Jim had always been the Big Brother to John and Bob. His not being able to have any sway over John, who's impulsiveness led to his death, remained a sorrow Jim would bear for the rest of his life.

"The tragic Northfield episode was, of course, a terrific shock to you and to me," Jim concluded. "Yet you hid your sorrow from the searching eyes of an inquisitive world.

"It mattered not that Justice was being served by our being behind prison walls. That same curious world endeavored to penetrate those walls and failed as we three were permitted our privacy. However, it did not prevent the perverted minds of dime novel writers from making us hunted, captured, despicable, desperate outlaws.

"You married as I urged you to. I could not think of you going on alone in what was helplessness of ever being pardoned. You have been widowed young. My constant prayer is that with your three children, there will be only happiness in the years ahead. I am confident you will carry on for the children, yourself and for me.

Con Amour,

Jim Younger"

But let's not get ahead in the story. Since the robbery at Northfield defined most of Jim's life, it is natural that he would want to tell his side of the events.

CHAPTER 7
Northfield

On August 16, 1898, Jim wrote to Cora Lee:

My dear Cora Lee,

As you have never questioned me regarding my unwill-
ing participation in the Northfield affair, or with whom
I made the trip north from Monagaw—to the finale—the
grim inhospitable gates of Stillwater Prison, this unsolicited account, my story of the Northfield affair, the other
side of the coin as I knew it, lived it and rode with it, will
come as a complete surprise to you.

Because of Cole's assuming to be the spokesman (self-
appointed) of our duo, you have always accepted his ver-
sions of the affair, without comment or proof of credibility.

While this is true, in Cole's defense, Jim never wanted to talk
about it to anyone. He "clamed up" from the get-go.

"Listening as Cole related or read his various conceptions
of the entire Northfield event to you Cora Lee and though
I never wholly agreed with him, simply letting it ride at
the time, without protesting his opinions, I created an error
that I have endured for years," Jim continues.

"I wanted no unpleasantness as friction to mar the close brotherly intimacy we had enjoyed all through life, that a gossip hungry world could misconstrue.

"Cole has intimated in years past, perhaps hopefully, that I not write of my Northfield experience. Until now, I have humored him without committing myself but since in his most recent version, as he related it to you, he credited me with riding north with him. I have reached the conclusion, now is the time for me to give you my side of that ill-fated expedition, as it does concern me personally.

"I did not ride north with either Cole or Bob, only from Monagaw Springs to Kansas City. When we rode out of the Springs, late in August of 1876, it was the first time in our adult life we three Youngers ever rode together."

Why Jim would begin his telling of his story to Cora Lee with this untruth rather sets the rest of his account in suspicion.

In Cole Younger's autobiography, he states that the entire party of the three Youngers, the two James boys, Clell Miller, Bill Stiles (also known as Bill Chadwell), and Charley Pitts boarded a train in Kansas City, bound for Minnesota. It has been said the men traveled as far as Council Bluff, Iowa. Yet many years later, Cole told his friend Harry Hoffman that they rode all the way to Northfield on horses from home.

"Cole and I were never in the same field of combat the short time I was in the Confederate service," Jim continues. "I was never involved in any of Cole's activities or with Bob. Cole and I hoped that some day we could pool our resources into stock breeding and raising in Texas. This was before Bob met Jesse James on the street in Kansas City. We gave up the project when we could not convince Bob that Jesse's harebrained scheme only meant trouble for all of us.

"Any one of Cole's explanations are all of his own egotistic concept. His reason for doing so is too deep for me to even guess the why, and in the passing years I have ceased to feel concern, only when it affects me adversely. Doubtless all three of us, Cole, Bob and I, each had his perception of the situation, yet never has the topic of the tragic event been discussed at any length.

"For the first time in my life I question the veracity of my brother Cole, although I would not admit it to anyone but you, Cora Lee. Bob is gone. I can prove none of my asserted narrative. I can only hope that you know I am stating the true facts as it happened to me."

Bob died on September 20, 1889, of consumption without ever giving his side of the "event." What follows is Jim's account of the Northfield robbery and the time and circumstances surrounding it. Much of what Jim says comes into question in regard to what we know after years of research into the robbery. It is possible that time and the deterioration of his mental health caused Jim to remember things differently. He certainly suffered from Post Tramatic Stress Disorder (PTSD), and those who suffer from this sometimes remember things incorrectly. It might be that some of Jim's revisionism is to "correct" those things he unconsciously "chose" to believe differently. Yet his story has some very interesting insights and some of his "facts" are worth examining.

"Remaining for so many years in Cole's shadow, my standard reply to all inquiries on any subject, has become a parrot-like phrase, 'Ask Cole,'" Jim writes. "But after more than twenty years, this old worm has broken out of his cocoon and though I will never became a brilliant raconteur, Deadwood Dick has nothing to fear from me. I will no longer be put off relating two incidents that affected me and wherein Cole did not participate in any way. I refer to John's death in 1874. He was only twenty-three at the time. And this, the truth of my ride from Kansas City, Mo. to Northfield, Minnesota in August of 1876,

"You may think, and rightfully so, as you read, I am interposing a volume of detail before reaching the salient part of my narrative. Later incidents will coincide each in its proper place, supporting my minute account, as being essential and factual to the entire affair as I lived it.

"If I am tedious, I apologize. To me the truth, as I will endeavor to relate it, is significantly important, even though it seems dull, lacks depth and imaginative literary technique.

"Should you compare this, my statement, with any of Cole's, numerous as they are, you may accuse me of being indefinite, even ambiguous at times but obviously there was no unusual episode to relate. The high lights of the entire ride north for me was the purchase of fresh mounts at Albert Lea and our meeting with Frank James' party, Thursday Sept. 7, 1876, which included my brothers Cole and Bob.

"Jesse, Stiles, Miller and I rode as unobtrusively as we could. There was no sightseeing, no gambling. I was never interested in cards as Cole and Bob were. If Jesse, Stiles and Miller were players, they never mentioned the fact.

"(I was a fair billiard player. Dr. McNeil was considered a brilliant billiard player and we played together at your home. Did I ever win? Cora Lee, I was matched against your father, remember?)"

Jim alludes to the men being divided into two groups: Jesse, Clell, Bill, and himself in one, and Frank, Cole, Bob, and Charlie in the other. That may have been so in the final days or hours but there was much intermingling prior to reaching Northfield. Jim doesn't mention anything about their travels after they arrive in the north, other than buying horses in Albert Lea.

The first town of any importance seems to be Minneapolis. Bob later recalled playing cards there in the company of Charlie Pitts, where the pair lost $200 and slept on the bank of the river rather than in a hotel to save money. The next day, the men traveled to St. Paul. Cole and Bill Stiles stayed at the Merchant Hotel on 3rd and Jackson Streets. They took to the gaming tables and won some money.

Jim, Clell, and the James brothers stayed at the Nicolette House outside St. Paul, an establishment run by Mollie Ellsworth, a well-liked madam. Stiles joined the quartet later. He was a friend of Kitty Traverse, who lived at the House. Apparently, Jim had been sent along to keep an eye on Jesse. Kitty Traverse later said one of the men was said to be ill and never left his room. This was likely Jim, who was both nervous about the upcoming event and far too pious to be seen in a house of ill repute. Cole joined them the next day, leaving Charlie and Bob in St. Paul.

On August 20, Bob and Charlie dropped by the Hall and McKinney Livery but were unable to purchase suitable horses. They did buy two McClellan saddles and a bridle. They then went by Norton & Ware, where they bought a bit. They finally found two horses they liked, Bob's being a Chestnut Bay, and bought them from William A. Judd on 4th Street. When the other six men returned to

St. Paul, a man resembling Jesse was seen purchasing a map in a bookstore and Bill Stiles apparently ran into Patrick Kenny of the St. Paul Police Force, who recognized Stiles from having arrested him years before on charges of stealing a horse.

It is believed that Jesse, Jim, Clell, and Frank James took the train to Red Wing, Minnesota, at this point. Jim's account would not have Frank James in this party, but rather Bill Stiles. They posed as cattle buyers and registered at the National Hotel. While there in Red Wing, they purchased three horses.

If we are to accept Jim's memory of the various parties, Bob stayed behind, either in the company of Bill Stiles or Charlie Pitts (likely Pitts, as the two were becoming friends). Cole took the train to St. Peter with either Stiles, Pitts, or Frank James. It was likely it was Stiles and that Frank was indeed with Jim, Clell, and Jesse makes sense as Frank and Jesse split from the group to travel to Brush Prairie. Once there, they pretended to buy a farm from John Mulligan, only so as to learn more about the nearby town of Northfield. They got out of the purchase by saying their money was in Red Wing and they would return. Cole, in the company of someone, according to Jim's account Frank James, also looked the town over.

"I became better acquainted with Pitts after the so-called raid failed," Jim says. "I have a deep sense of appreciation for his unselfish loyalty to Cole, Bob and I."

Charlie Pitts actually knew the Youngers as a boy. He was first at the scene of their father's murder. Jim may not have remembered him from that.

"For years it seems to me, Cole delights in telling of his party's carefree, playboy attitude; his conversations with various people, hotel owners—as the four made their way north," Jim continues.

"In contrast, as I have stated, we four—Jesse, Miller, Stiles and I—attracted no attention as we rode, doubtless each man contemplating his unknown, unforeseeable future, containing his dreams, desires and hopes. I experienced all this, including regret, as I lengthened the miles from my loved ones.

The Old Fool,

Jim Younger"

Jim continued his account in his next letter:

From where they, Frank's party, were coming, I did not ask then or since. I do not know. At the time, from my viewpoint, it mattered little as to how or when they arrived, or left, any particular place. I had not been with them so did not concern myself.

Something critical is missing here in Jim's recollections. He gives no mention of the group's visit to the town of Mankato, where Jesse first considered the possibility of robbing that town's bank. Cole went into great detail of this possibility and the trip to that area in his account of what happened in Minnesota. First, he claimed that Jesse had suggested Mankato rather than Northfield but because the farmers had already suffered from the recent grasshopper attack they didn't think it would be the thing to do. In other accounts, he says that when they got to Mankato to check it out, Jesse thought someone had recognized him on the street.

That at least some of the men were present in Mankato cannot be denied. Cole and Charlie passed through the nearby area of Hanska and stopped at the farmhouse of Mads and Grenhild Ouren. They ended up staying the night, and Cole admired Mad's "fine gun" that hung over the kitchen door. (In later days, reunited once again, Ouren and Cole would remember the exchange.) Then Cole and Charlie rode to Madelia, where they stayed at the Flanders Hotel. Here, Cole and owner Thomas Vought had a friendly conversation that both men would later recall as well.

All the men gathered together in Mankato, two staying at the Clifton House, two staying at the Gates House, and the others elsewhere. When the bank robbery was aborted, the men rode out of town.

The group split again. Three of them—Cole, Bob, and Charlie—and a fourth (Cole said Frank) stayed in the Johnson House in Janesville on September 4. Cole later wrote that the day after, they were in Le Sueur Center and their night sleep was disturbed because court was in session and the town was full of people. However, the town of Cleveland was the county seat of Le Sueur County and if the court was indeed in session, Cole noted the wrong town.

The other group laid up in Waterville the night of September 5. Some people in that town later said that a man answering Jesse's description was told to leave town, under the belief that he was someone else. That night Cole's group stayed at the Dampier House in Cordova. They were forced to share a room with a man named W. W. Barlow as the hotel was filled to capacity.

On September 6, one group stayed at the farm of C. C. Stetson on the old Faribault Road outside of Northfield, while the other stayed at the Cushman Hotel in Millersburg.

"We met Frank's party some three to five miles southwest of Northfield," wrote Jim. "All were well mounted. Naturally I was interested in and even critical of the horses they rode. Cole mounted on a big chested dapple-gray. As

I have mentioned before, Cole was a large man. He needed a big, sturdy, sure-footed animal with stamina to carry his, Cole's, well over two hundred pounds.

"Frank rode a fractious red bay, well built but would need a firm hand to control its passage propensity. It would probably bolt in an emergency."

As was determined later, during the robbery, Frank was riding a dun horse.

"Pitts was astride a sturdy, fairly quiet pinto that showed speed and endurance," Jim continued.

"Bob's mount was a beautiful chestnut. No other color of horse appealed to him. To me it seemed a bit restless. Bob would call it 'ginger' that he liked in a horse and could handle in his gentle way. It was a splendid looking animal. I was proud of Bob's judgment of horseflesh.

"There was not the slightest indication of brotherly affection between Frank and Jesse when they met. No word of greeting. Cole, Bob and I only had time for a grinning 'howdy' before Jesse asked Frank and Cole how the town looked to them. (Oh how I hoped the answer would be 'not good.') but Frank said 'middlin' quiet' and for once Cole was silent, willing to let Frank explain perhaps.

"Frank went on to say, 'We all rode through town, located this road you all would be comin' on, then went back to town. Bud and me ate in one place; Bob and Charley ate down the street apiece. After dinner me and Bud walked around town, found the bank. It ain't very big and ain't on a corner, like Joe said.' (I had never heard of Joe and by Cole's expression, neither had he.)

"From the amazed look on Jesse's face as he listened to Frank, I expected a violent outburst of his ungovernable temper. We were all relieved when he said 'Ate your dinners in town,' adding sarcastically 'Then you two numbskulls took in the town.'

"There was no comment from anyone. I, for once, was in full accord with Jesse. Never having been in the robbery business, I had not the slightest inkling of how to lay the proper groundwork preceding a robbery, bank or otherwise.

"It did occur to me Frank James could establish first hand information, authentic and indisputable. Judging by the expression on Jesse's face, he was of the same opinion.

"Cole and Bob, like me, were absolutely no help, just a trio of illiterates on the subject. Personally I was quite happy, blissfully so, in my ignorance. "

Cole, in fact, had plenty of experience on the topic. Not only had he participated in other robberies, he had been a scout during the war and part of his job description was sousing out various locations. Back to Jim:

As Frank continued his explanation to Jesse, he was drawing a diagram on the ground under the trees. We all watched and listened. He indicated Northfield's two main streets, showing the bank's location relative to the one street intersection, about a third of a mile farther along the road we came in on, which Frank said would be Main Street, after crossing the wagon bridge spanning the Cannon River, a short distance from our camp and on east, beyond the crossroad.

Frank also indicated a two-story building, facing west on Division at the southeast corner of the intersection. The lower floor was a general store, Lee and Hitchcock. He was rather vague about it. Around the corner, west on Main, adjoining to the building, was an open staircase, balustered with a grill balcony at the upper floor landing.

Farther along on Main Street was the bank entrance, facing north. Perhaps a hundred feet from the stairway and on further east.

It seems that Jim was giving this detailed description of the area to show that he had, indeed, been there. He might have hoped that by his being so precise, it would give his further account more credibility.

" It was after one o'clock by the time Jesse, Frank and Cole rounded out their programs from Frank's depictions, " Jim continues. "Frank, Pitts and Bob were to ride up Main Street, directly to the tie rack. (This [is] the first mention of their being a tie rack being anywhere near the bank. I had ample course to learn of its location later, between the bank and the stairway but closer to the door of the bank.)

"The three, Frank, Pitts and Bob, were to dismount and tie, then wait until Cole and Miller, following about two blocks behind them, were near enough to protect the three, should anything go wrong before they entered the bank.

"Jesse, Stiles and I were to wait at the west end of the bridge, not crossing unless Cole fired once in the air, mean-ing trouble and we were to ride in. The boys, at Cole's signal, were to leave the bank, get mounted and ride out of town.

"If no alarm was given, supposing all went well, the same procedure was to be followed. By the time the three came out, Cole would have finished adjusting his gear, Miller waiting for him. Both would ride on together.

"Jesse, Stiles and I were to turn back toward Faribault to the road, by-passing that town, as we did earlier in the day. I described the turn-off as best I could and it was agreed we would all meet somewhere on that back road."

There has always been speculation as to who it was who entered the bank. It seems unusual that the ever-controlling Jesse would choose not to be an active part of the robbery and instead stay so far behind the initial action. If we are to believe Jim, it was Frank James, Bob Younger, and Charlie Pitts.

"There was to be no shooting, only in the event of unexpected self defense," Jim goes on. "Jesse's orders, strangely enough.

"Frank, Pitts and Bob rode leisurely across the bridge, and on up Main Street, crossed Division, turned to the tie rack and dismounted. They were then out of our sight beyond the horses. I am sure Jesse was wondering what they were doing, just as I was."

Bob, Charlie, and Frank (or was it Bob, *Jesse*, and Frank) ate their lunch at a restaurant across from the bank. About 1:50 p.m, they walked over to sit on some dry goods boxes that were stacked in front of Lee & Hitchcock's store.

"Cole and Miller had waited until the two were about two blocks from us before they walked their horses across the bridge," remembered Jim. "Jesse, Stiles and I remained on the west side. Suddenly Stiles' chestnut mount sidled across the bridge, Stiles making no effort to control it. Only when across he brought it gently to stand. Neither Jesse or I questioned his action, nor did Bill offer an explanation, or even look in our direction. For several days previous I had thought Stiles himself was restless. It's a pity, so few people know that in some ways a horse is more sensitive than a dog and reacts more quickly to the mood of the rider than one realizes. The back and forth movement of a horses' ears, twitching of his muzzle, the shake of his head, all convey to the rider many things. Evidently Stiles was unaware he was communicating his unease to his mount.

"Jesse and I, mounted, waited on the north side of the road. From there we had an unobstructed view east, along Main Street, to the bank entrance, beyond where the horses were tied, but we still could not see what the men were doing.

"Cole and Miller were at least a block from the bank when the three men appeared at the horses' heads on the sidewalk in single file, headed toward the bank, Frank James leading, then Pitts, then Bob."

When Cole and Clell Miller saw the three men sitting on the boxes, Cole also noticed there were quite a few people around. Cole said he mentioned this to Clell and wondered why the men hadn't just ridden through town when they saw so many people. It was now 2:00 p.m. Miller told him, "They are going in." Cole replied, "If they do, the alarm will be given as sure as there's a hell, so you better take that pipe out of your mouth."

"As we watched, Cole and Miller, as yet some distance from the three on the walk, Jesse remarked impatiently,

'What ails Frank? Is he daft?'" Jim continued. "Had I the time, or been so inclined, I doubt if my detailed adjective-filled (descriptively) reply would have contained the least semblance of rationality in either Mr. Wood, Mr. Howard or our entire outfit. In my limited brain, we were all daft. Please note, Cora Lee, Jesse used the name 'Frank' not 'Buck.'

"On reaching the door to the bank, Frank seemed to open it and entered, followed by Pitts. Bob being last turned and looked down the street toward Cole and Miller, still on their leisurely stroll, seemingly totally oblivious to the three men entering the bank. Bob paused only an instant, then he too entered but he did not close the door.

"As Cole and Miller reached their planned positions, Miller, riding on Cole's left, rode ahead a few paces, I judged almost opposite the open door. Reining in, he turned, looking back at Cole as though waiting. Cole had dismounted, standing beside his horse when he was fired upon. Dropping the reins, he ran to the door, paused, waving his arms, then ran back to his mount. As he toed the stirrup, a shot was fired over his head, as he drew his revolver to fire the warning signal. Stiles took off, not waiting for Cole to fire.

"As Jesse and I galloped up the street after Stiles, I saw Miller dismount, run to the bank's open door. I thought he was urging the boys to come out. Then he reached in, and to my amazement he pulled the door forward, closing it. Why? With the three men inside? I learned later, Cole called to Miller to 'Get the boys out, close the door.' Did Cole expect Miller to stand at the door, a prime target, until they came out? Only Cole knew the why. He has never explained."

As the citizens of Northfield began to realize what was happening, they grabbed whatever weapons they could find and began the attempt to defend their town's bank. Cole continued to fire into the air as he shouted out to the citizens to get off the street. "Get off the damn street!" he yelled as a weaponless man named Nicholas Gustavson wandered toward him. As the man continued forward he was shot, likely caught in the crossfire but probably not by Cole.

"Galloping up the street, behind Stiles, I could see him holding to the middle of the street, pass Cole on his (Cole's) left, pull up about midway between Cole and Miller's horse," Jim continues. "I rode to Cole's right, glanced at Stiles, who as yet was not using his gun although there was an occasional shot from a citizen aimed at no one in particular.

"Stiles sat apparently staring at Miller. As he {Miller} turned, after closing the door, and ran toward his horse, he was shot. His face was riddled as though someone was firing an old blunderbuss. Miller fell, face down, a step from his ground-tied sorrel that had turned, bringing his left side toward Miller. I am sure Miller died instantly."

Elias Stacy shot Clell Miller in the face with a small-caliber fowling piece. J. S. Allen was in his store, handing out guns and ammunition to anyone who would take them and had given the gun to Stacy.

"I was so shocked that all thought of Stiles left me," claims Jim. "I have no recollection of seeing him again. After Miller fell, there was a few seconds lull from the citizens which Cole took advantage of by tossing his reins to me. Dismounting, he ran to the bank door, flung it open shouting 'Bob, you idiot. Come out.' Hearing the door open he ran back to remount.

"This action seemed to revive the townsmen as they opened up a heavier barrage in our direction. I fired two shots in the air. As Cole toed his stirrup, he lurched, almost losing his balance. Grasping the pommel with his left hand and the cantle with his right, he regained the hull.

"By the expression on his face, as he settled in the saddle, I knew he had been shot. I said, 'You have been hit. Where?' Reaching for the reins I held out to him he said, 'Don't think about it now. Get Bob out of there. He won't listen to me.'"

Anselm Manning, who owned a hardware store, shot at Cole but missed. After he reloaded he shot again, this time shooting Bill Stiles through the heart as he sat atop his horse. Stiles fell to the ground, dead.

"I had just grounded my reins and dismounted when Bob dashed out the door, turned toward the tie rack," writes Jim. "He staggered a bit, drew his revolver, but did not fire. His right arm hung limp and I knew he had been shot. His right hand was useless. His draw had been a swift, cross motion of his left arm and hand.

"Bob was the only one in our family who was ambidextrous but he never wore but one gun, holstered on his right hip but never tied down, his theory being the same as Cole's and mine. A thong-downed gun was the mark of a killer. A killer Bob was not."

Jim seems to imply that Bob was shot shortly after leaving the bank. In fact, as Bob ran down the street, he encountered Manning. He ducked under a staircase and the two men exchanged fire. Henry Wheeler fired at Bob from a second story window across the street, hitting and shattering Bob's elbow.

"Watching as Bob neared the horses at the rack, I saw they were rearing and plunging," continues Jim. "Then Bob's horse broke its reins below the bit rings and galloped down the street. Even though Bob was afoot, it was not his nature to take one of the remaining two horses for his use—leaving Frank or Pitts stranded.

"I was about to mount and go to Bob, when Miller's horse, I suppose sensing a companion in my Black, whinnied softly and with his head turned sideways to avoid the reins, sidled toward me—a mount for Bob. I sprinted to the oncoming sorrel, ducking instinctively, as bullets whistled over my head. At that moment, Pitts ran out the bank door and turned left, toward the rack. Catching up the reins of the sorrel, I led him back to Bob. Pitts, mounted, was backing his pinto away from the rack. Helping Bob into the saddle, I heard Cole yell 'Charley.' Turning my head, I saw Pitts scrambling to get out of his saddle as his pinto went down. Cole again shouted 'Go up the street, Pitts and I'll pick you up.' Pitts passed us on the run, firing once in the air. Several doors east, he was out of the direct line of fire, as he waited for Cole."

Cole recalled this differently. He told his friend Harry Hoffman that even though he was shot twice doing it, he reached down and grabbed Bob, pulling him up on his (Cole's) saddle.

"Turning from Bob to go around my Black to mount, Jesse on Frank's bay, leading his own buckskin on his right, rode between Bob and the building headed toward the bank door," continued Jim. "As he passed he yelled, 'Better get these nags on the road.' Riding on, he pulled up at the open door, shouting at Frank I suppose, who was the only one of the three still in the bank.

"(I have wondered many times just where was Jesse James during all the savage, cold-blooded uproar, the net result of his vicious scheme? Was he around the corner on Division Street, safely out of gun range, perhaps? Who knows?)

"As I settled in my saddle I was shot in the left shoulder. It felt like a large bullet and from the angle it ran it could have come from the balcony at the top of the stairs. Stunned, I tried to tell Bob to ride on, but I could not speak, as another lull in the citizen's barrage occurred."

Jim was shot by Henry Wheeler, although Wheeler claimed that it was before he shot Clell Miller.

"In that short interval of silence, two shots were fired in the bank, very close together," Jim writes. "The moment of silence continued, the citizens doubtless as surprised as our remaining five were.

"Jesse broke the silence, with more of his insensate shouting, again directed through the bank's open door. This seemed to signal the townsmen to resume bombardment.

"Bob and I, intent on joining Cole and Charley Pitts, crowded against Jesse to avoid Miller's body, just as Frank appeared in the doorway. Frank James, the first of the three men to enter the bank was now the last of the same three to come out.

"Giving out with the old Rebel yell, Frank leaped astride the buckskin from the right side as Bob and I urged our mounts ahead, hoping to ride out of the direct line of fire, each steel shod of our mounts striking the hard packed earth street, increasing our agony.

"Frank and Jesse passed us, Frank a revolver in each hand, raking both sides of the street with bullets, narrowly missed Cole and Pitts, turning off Main, Bob and I close on the gray's heels.

"Another turn or two brought the four of us back to Main Street, two blocks west of Division, headed for the bridge spanning the river. Clattering across, we were back on the Faribault road, Cole's big chested gray setting the mile eating pace with its long, springy stride evincing the fact it's stamina and bottom could carry double a long way before tiring.

"Never before, Cora Lee, had I allowed a horse to cross a bridge, either while riding or driving, only at a walk. It just isn't the thing to do. Also very few horses take kindly to being mounted from the right side (unless trained as the Indians do theirs) without giving the rider trouble. Yet Frank took that chance, against the buckskin's inherent tendency.

"Two or three miles beyond the river, Frank rode out of the brush and hailed us. We followed him to where Jesse waited. No one bothered to ask how they got ahead of us. Resting only a few minutes, to let the horses blow, we rode on a few miles and met a man driving a team hitched to a loaded hayrack. A sway-backed horse ambled at the side of the rack. Cole bargained with the man for the horse, insisting the halter, rope and two old feed sacks be included in the thirty-dollar deal. Cole wrote a bill of sale on the back of one he had in his pocket. The man signed it and drove on."

The man with the horse, hauling rails rather than hay, was Philip Empey. And it's likely the horse was procured for Bob. It's questionable whether Cole paid for the horse or wrote a receipt.

"Neither Jesse or Frank made any effort to pay for the poor old thing," claims Jim. "Pitts was grateful and said, 'It sure beats walking.'

"As Pitts made the change, Frank noticed that Stiles was not with us. 'Hey,' he shouted. 'Where's Bill. Anybody know? Was he killed? Did they nab him or what happened?'

"Pitts scrambling to mount was the only one to reply to Frank's inquiry saying, 'It's this way, Buck. After Bob run out, you was jawin' with one of the bank tellers. I yelled at you to come on, you paid me no mind so I lit out. Clell was lyin' in the road—dead. I guess Jim was pickin' up Clell's horse. Bill wasn't in sight and I sure had no time to look him up.'

"I could have said I saw him, as I rode up to Cole, saw him a brief moment as he watched Miller. The next moment Bill Stiles was completely obliterated from my mind as I witnessed helplessly the horrible death of Clell Miller. I saw no reason to enlighten the James boys of what little I knew of Stiles' actions at the time, neither have I commented upon him since, until now.

"Bill Stiles did not appear at our trial as a defendant. He was never identified at any time as having been captured or killed. So far as I know Cole has no knowledge of him either."

It is possible that Jim did not see Stiles shot or lying dead on the ground. Yet in the many years passed since the incident, it is curious that Jim would not have read or heard that Stiles was left dead on the street in Northfield.

CHAPTER 8

The Retreat

It was now time for the Gang to get out of Northfield. Only $26.70 had been removed from the First National Bank of Northfield, money that Bob Younger had gathered from the counter.

"I had missed the turn off I had suggested earlier, so we rode on for several miles, always on the lookout for a secluded place to stop," continues Jim. "Pitts spotted a small stand of timber and brush off the road some distance and we turned toward our first real stop. The weather had changed, turned colder, threatening rain. Cole, Bob and I were suffering intensely and our mounts needed to blow and rest."

This stop was likely after they passed through Dundas and Millersburg. By this time, Mayor J. T. Ames had called for a posse and the request was well met. Jim continues his story without mentioning the several days of the group's escape. He even implies that the band of outlaws was only together for one day after the robbery. The flight of the men in the days following the event is well documented.

Two posse scouts spotted the exchange with Philip Empey on the Dundas Road and trailed the group. After they procured a horse, the outlaws stopped at the farm of Robert Donaldson for a pail of water to cleanse Bob's wound. When Donaldson asked how Bob had been injured, he was told the group had been in a fight with a "Blackleg" in Northfield and that Bob had been shot. But all was well, as the Blackleg had been killed. When Donaldson asked the Blackleg's name, he was told "Stiles."

They stopped again near Shieldsville to use a water pump that stood outside a saloon to water horses. An old man watched them as they pumped the water but became more curious when Bob, who had been fighting consciousness, fell off his horse. As they dragged Bob back up on his horse, Jesse informed the man that Bob was a horse thief and they were taking him to be hung. The old man shrugged and went inside the saloon. Four curious men very quickly emerged from the saloon after having been informed of the questionable men outside. The outlaws drew their guns as they retreated into the woods.

Fourteen others soon joined the men from the saloon as they chased the ragtag group but the outlaws were able to enter the Big Woods area and hide themselves as a torrential rain began. The rain would continue on and off over the next two weeks. At the time of this incident, there were already 200 men in the field looking for the outlaws. By the next day, September 8, there would be 300 more. Later that day, two men, probably Frank and Jesse rode up to the farm of George James near Waterville. They said they were looking for two lost mules and wondered about the condition of the area near the river. As they rode down the Cordova road, they encountered a small group of men who had been working on the road and had stopped to shelter themselves from the rain. The outlaws asked where they might cross the river and were told there was a bridge further down the road. As the men approached the bridge however, they spotted a posse that had been formed by a Captain

Rodgers. They passed the bridge, going around Tetonka Lake only to come face to face with the posse on the other side. As shooting began, the gang spurred their horses into the lake, crossing over and disappearing into the surrounding woods.

As they headed to Janesville later in the afternoon, they took two horses from farmer John Laney and two from Ludwig Rosenau. They ordered Rosenau's son Wilhelm to lead them to where they could cross the river safely. Traveling to Le Sueur County, the men stopped at the farm of a family named Rosenhall. Here, they forced two boys to relinquish their plowing horses and guide them to the Elysian Road. They went on to Waterville, where they left their horses and two of the men were able to procure some food.

On September 9, Governor J. S. Pillsbury of Minnesota offered a $1,500 dead or alive reward for the men who robbed the North-field bank. On September 10, over 200 posse members at Lake Elysian surrounded the outlaws. The Gang was able to hide on an island and elude the posse. They tied up their horses and continued on foot. The next day they camped one mile west of the lake. They spent the next day and a half at a deserted farm four miles northeast of Mankato.

On September 12, they left the farm but crossed paths with a farmhand named Thomas "Jeff" Dunning. There was some debate over what should be done with a man who could tell a posse where they were, should Dunning be allowed to go on his way. Cole didn't like the idea of killing the man or tying him to a tree where his being hidden by the woods might make it impossible for him to be found and where he would die anyway. Eventually, they threatened Dunning that there would be dire consequences if he were to tell of their whereabouts and they set him free. They then passed by the farm of L. M. Demarary and stole some of his chickens. Dunning tried to keep to his bargain with the outlaws but when Dunning was found by his friends to be acting strangely, they continued to question him as to what was wrong. After three hours, Dunning spilled the beans. But by that time, the outlaws were long gone, having crossed the Blue Earth River at a railroad bridge and following the rails around the town of Mankato. They stopped to rest outside Mankato. They had only traveled fifty miles since they left Northfield.

Jim picks up the story at this point.

Reaching the scant, but welcome, shelter of the grove, Frank, Jesse and Pitts dismounted, Cole and I remaining in our saddles, unable to dismount alone, until Pitts, realizing we both were badly injured, came to our assistance. Bob slid off the sorrel like a small boy, belly fashion. Pitts then loosened the cinches for us. Neither Mr. Woods or Mr. Howard showed any inclination to lend a helping hand.

As Jesse finished loosening the cinch on his bay, he turned and faced me, his belt held in his right hand. The square, highly polished metal Confederate buckle he still affected loomed large. Many of us who had worn them during the war had long since discarded them, as a remnant of a bitter memory of a war hopefully over and best forgotten. To Jesse, it may have been a fetish of magic powers, preserving him from injury, deserving a special devotion in all our riding together. I had given the buckle no thought till then.

Jesse gave his belt a tug, causing his holster to flap against his right hip, indicating it was empty. I gave him a quick, once over glance, but saw no evidence of a hidden holstered gun.

The set of Cole's jaw proved he was suffering and he was also furious. Leaning against a tree, to ease the pain in his hip, Bob supporting him on his right, Cole vehemently began questioning Frank. "Buck," he said. "I want to know why you fellows went into the bank before Miller and I rode up. What caused the shooting in the bank after Pitts and Bob came out. Who did it and why."

Frank started to speak but was interrupted by Jesse, intimating loudly it was none of Cole's business what Buck did. Cole cut him off sharply, saying "I am making it my business and I am not asking you for your opinion, so shut up until I do." Cole, looking directly at Frank, went on to say, "Well, Buck?" Even though he spoke softly there was an edge to his tone, decidedly menacing.

Before answering Cole, Frank unbuttoned his shirt, drew an ornate handled .44 from the waist band of his pants, handed it butt first to Jesse saying, "Reckon I better give this back to you, Dingus. Its empty, better load it." Dingus' only comment, as he slipped the .44 into his empty holster was, "Sure, Buck." He still held his belt in his hand.

A rocket seemed to explode in my brain. The theory to which I had given my random speculation was a fully proven fact. The seventeen days I had been riding north with Jesse James, that same ornate .44 had been holstered on his right hip, yet now it was being handed nonchalantly by Buck to his brother Dingus.

Adding these incidents to the recent sinister demonstration by Buck, I not only witnessed but was a near casualty on the main street of Northfield, convinced me I had stumbled onto what was doubtless a here-to-fore closely guarded James' secret. Frank James was a pistoleer par excellence.

Personally, I knew nothing of the man, only by here-say. I had never been interested in either he or Jesse, to inquire to their capabilities or mode of living.

The meeting this morning was the second time I had met him. On both occasions I had noticed he wore only one holstered gun, a .45, I judged. (This was later confirmed by Frank's own statement as a Colt .45.)

Today, with his Colt .45, ably assisted by Jesse's ornate .44, Buck Woods, the well known Frank James, had unwittingly exhibited his two-gun ability. Never would he conceal that fact by the wearing of only one gun, holstered, either sinister or dexter.

Again, Jim claims to have only known Frank since the morning of the robbery, which he mentions as "this morning."

"I realize I have digressed from my narrative. I do so rather than resort to fiction instead of the factual, as I have so often heard Cole do in his egotistic descriptions of his personal exploits, recounted to you," Jim writes.

"My comments so far expressed on the conduct and character (personalities) of Frank and Jesse James are my own conclusions based on the association of less than one day with Frank and seventeen days riding and camping with Jesse. I had had no previous interest in, or any acquaintance with either man, only when Cole had his troubles with Jesse and mentioned Frank or Jesse in that I had no part.

"I do not wish my observations to be regarded in any way as being antagonistic toward Frank and Jesse James because of the failure of their wild scheme, that dream bubble of easy wealth, that had burst so violently. (Cole and I did not ride north for a share of the money possibility involved, but to protect Bob. We failed to accomplish that.)

"I do hope to expose the shocking apathetic attitude displayed by Frank and Jesse of the entire affair, to the death of one of their friends, our injuries, our fault for being there and to Frank shooting the cashier, Jesse for his proposal and insinuations as to Bob.

"Little wonder my chaotic impressions resembled a kaleidoscope without color. At each turn of the mental instrument, all the pieces fell into one symmetrical whole as I, filled with grim emotion and foreboding, waited with the others in silence for Frank to answer the questions demanded by my brother, Thomas Coleman Younger.

"It is not my intention to give the impression that the following is Frank James exact wordage. It is as I interpreted the gist of his detailed explanations of the affair at the time. And while Cole, Bob and I never discussed any phase of his story with each other, I am aware of the facts, as I have given them are, as Cole heard Frank's account, except when Cole talked to you, Cora Lee, he changed the names of the men who went into the bank."

Cole always claimed it was Bob Younger, Charlie Pitts, and Jesse James who went into the bank. Naming Jesse was relieving his friend Frank James from the heat. Also, it seems rather strange to think that the three Younger brothers never discussed the robbery with each other. Why would that be?

I have nothing to gain, or lose, by any statement I have made, or will make. I shall not live long enough. What I have written, use as you wish or deem best.

I wish to emphasize what I feel was the callous indifference to all that had occurred so recently in Northfield, as evinced by Frank's attitude all through his account. As he arrogantly addressed himself directly to Cole, the two could have been in a world apart from the five of us who were listening. For myself, I was appalled.

Interesting that Jim claims *five* men listening instead of four. Here, he begins relating what Frank claimed had occurred:

"Well, Bud, it was like this," Frank began. "When we split up to eat dinner in different places, Bud you went on ahead of me. Charley wanted to borrow the price of a slug of whiskey." Bob said, "Jesse and Bud won't like that, Charley and I'll pay for your dinner." Charley said, "One drink never bothered me yet, besides we haven't met them yet so they won't know what I had."

Well, I gave him all the money I had. He owes me a dollar six bits. I was sure Bud, you would pay for my dinner, Bud, like you and Bob been doing knowing I was broke.

"Well, Bud," Frank went on, "I guess he bought the stuff while you and me was looking the town over and I reckon he drank about half off it before we met Dingus."

When we was squatted down between the horses, there at the hitch rack, Charley got a bottle out of his hip pocket and started to pass it around. Bob said, "No, I told you I don't drink the stuff." And you know I don't either, Bud. I reckon the bottle was about half full anyway. Charley finished it off and pitched the bottle out in the street.

Cole later wrote to Dr. A. E. Hedback that indeed one of the men had secured a bottle of whiskey and that he—maybe all three of his companions—had drunk it before the robbery. Cole said that the whiskey was responsible for the botched robbery and had he known there was liquor involved he would never have entered the town. He would later suggest—after the death of Bob—that Bob had been drinking but this is unlikely. It's hard to understand why he would throw his brother under the bus except to perhaps make his story more credible in the retelling and to make it clear to his listeners that he was in no way to blame for what happened.

"Cole showed his impatience as he said, 'I still don't see why you didn't follow the plan you, Jesse and I worked out,'" Jim continues.

"'I just got tired squatting there waiting,' Frank said peevishly. 'So I got up to see what was holding you and Miller up. You were down the road quite apiece, poking along like you had all day. So then I took a good squint all around. Wasn't anybody paying us any mind so I says, "Boys, this is it. We go in now."'

" 'Bob and Charley got up,' Frank went on. 'Bob looked down the road, saw you fellows ambling your nags along like you was riding snails and he says, "Jesse and Cole won't like that." I got sort of riled and said, "Just what can they do about it if we get the job done quiet like? By the time them two get here, if they ever do, we can have the job over, ready to skedaddle before anybody knows it."'

"Cole was still persistent saying, 'I don't see as yet why you went ahead. It don't make sense to me.' Frank stared at Cole a moment, as though he pitied Cole's denseness in not grasping the situation as he, Frank, had explained it.

"Frank's tone was contentious as he spoke sharply, still apparently speaking only to Cole. 'Like I said, I was tired squatting there like a toad, waiting for you fellows. The time looked good to me, so I made up my own mind. You know, Bud, this isn't the first bank I ever held up and I know the business. You don't, and so far I've never asked any help from you. I didn't ask you to come on this one. You come on your own, so what gives you the notion you know so all-fired much about how to rob a bank?'"

Again, Jim attempts to convince that Cole's participation in the Northfield robbery was his first bank job. He mentions nothing of Cole's involvement in the bank robberies that occurred in Liberty, St. Genevieve in Missouri, and Huntington, West Virginia.

"Cole threw his hands up in a gesture of surrender, saying, 'Nothing, of course,'" Jim continues. "'I was just plain stupid not to have noticed something was wrong before you boys rode up the street. The deal would never had gone on without the three Youngers taking part. Buck, you and Jesse both know we three agreed before we started there was to be no drinking by anyone on this trip. Get on with your part in what happened after the three of you got in the bank.'

"Frank could not conceal his surprise at Cole's calm yet positive attitude and for a bit seemed at a loss for words or just where to resume his narrative.

"I am sure the others, Jesse, Charley and Bob sensed the tenseness of the momentary silence, as I did, knowing Cole and his ever ready unexcitable reaction to any event, expected or not. Frank James must have realized that he had stretched the limit of Cole's patience.

"When he resumed his explanation, his tone of voice indicated he had lost much of his self-confidence, as he said, 'Well, I was sure I had it all worked out. You and Clell weren't so close that folks would figure we knew you, not the way you poked along. I could see the bank door was shut so I said this is how we do it. When we get in, you fellows hold back. I do the talking and like Dingus said, no shooting. Last one in, leave the door open.

"'Me and Charley starts off and Bob hung back and I could see he didn't want to go until you got there so I said, "Make up your mind, Sprout. Coming or not?" and he fell in behind Charley. We got to the door, I opened it and went in first, then Charley and Bob and he left the door open like I said to do.

"'Well when we got inside,' Frank went on, 'the boys stood back like I told them, near the door.

"'There was a counter part way 'cross the front. Where we went in, it rounded and went back to some office. I reckon I saw the safe ran along the wall where the stores would be on the counter. The safe door was shut and a clock was on the wall.

"'There was a cage where the counter rounded and a man was there. Another fellow was at a desk on the side toward the offices. I ask the man in the cage if he was the cashier. He shook his head "no" and said, "See Mr. Heywood." I think that was what he said anyway. He pointed to an older man at a desk at the short end of the counter under the clock. I moved along the counter a ways. The man met me, said "Howdy. What can I do for you?" I said, "You can open that safe."

"'Well,' Frank continued, 'Mr. Heywood looked at the clock and said, "I can't do it. It takes two keys." I thought he was joshing and said, "I never heard of such a thing. How come?" Then I says, "Where are the two keys?" and he says, "Well, I got one" and he went on to say mister somebody or other, I don't remember his name. But anyway, he was home to dinner and wouldn't be back until one-thirty. It was only one o'clock. He had the other key. I told him I thought he was lying.'"

This idea of a second key is very interesting. It has long been established that the safe was on a new device called a time lock and that the cashier told the outlaws that it could only be opened during a certain time of the day and not disengaged before that time.

"'Then I heard a big to-do outside,' Frank continued. 'Guns blasting off and you, Bud, yelling at the door for us to come out. Sure I heard all the commotion but I wasn't about to leave before I got what I rode seventeen days for. I got out my knife and climbed up on the counter, squatted down in front of the old man, told him I would cut his throat if he didn't open the safe. But the old man just shook his head, kept on saying it wasn't possible without the other key.'"

Here, either Frank or Jim leave out some important details as to what went on inside the bank. The other employees in the bank were Clerk Frank J. Wilcox and Alonzo E. Bunker, the assistant bookkeeper.

Frank James stepped over to examine the vault and its lock at this point. Cashier Heywood moved forward quickly to attempt to shove Frank into the vault. Bob moved forward to grab Heywood and throw the man to the ground. Bob was supposed to be guarding Bunker but seeing the robbery was being derailed turned his attention to the bills and coins on the counter, which he began to stuff into his pockets. Seeing that Bob had been distracted, Bunker made a dash for the back door. Bob shot at Bunker, hitting him in the shoulder. Bunker propelled himself out the door, yelling "They're robbing the bank! Help!"

Frank dragged Heywood over to the vault demanding that he open it. He pointed the gun away from Heywood's ear and fired a shot into the floor.

Jim continues Frank's account:

Then Clell yelled, "Buck, get a move on." I couldn't hear all the rest he said with all the hullabaloo going on outside, yelling and shooting. Then he closed the door. Bob yelled, "Come on, Frank, you heard Cole's and Clell's warning." I heard the door open and slam shut. I knew he was gone.

I was still telling the old man off, Frank continued, when Charley let out a bellow. "Buck, I'm getting out of here" and he took off. I reckon he was the one left the door open. Frank paused a moment, glanced at Jesse, then continued. I was closing my knife, sliding off the counter, when the old man ducked down and came up with an old pistol, which I could see was no peashooter.

He was holding it with both hands, shaking like he had the ague and trying to sight it on me and I was sure he was about to blow me to kingdom come and me not exactly ready to make the trip.

Frank paused again, looked at Cole intently saying, "You know me, Bud. I always say never draw a gun unless you intend to use it, so I ups with old Betsy Colt and says, 'O.K, Mister, you want to play rough, I can oblige.' I reckon we triggered about the same time. Him being wobbly, his shot went wild and missed me. He dodged, so maybe I got him in the left shoulder."

That's not the way Clerk Wilcox remembered it. He said that the "last robber" mounted a desk at the front and as he turned to go, shot at Heywood. The shot missed. According to Wilcox, Heywood dodged behind his desk or sank into his chair, with his back next to the wall. Wilcox said that "As the robber made over the desk railing he turned, and placing his revolver to Heywood's head, fired." Wilcox makes no mention of a gun held or fired by Heywood. Those who witnessed the scene described blood and brains all over Heywood's desk. Hardly something that could be misconstrued as a possible shoulder wound.

"'Well, anyway,'" Frank continued per Jim, "'nobody else raised any rumpus in the place as he dropped, so I made tracks for the door. Dingus was there yelling at me fit to bust a lung and on my bay, leading his buckskin. So I let go the old Rebel yell to scare the daylight out of them Yankees doing all the shooting, straddled the buckskin and me and Dingus took off up the road, went by Jim and the Sprout like they were standing still and that's all there was to it, Bud.'

"Was the breathless silence that followed Frank James' concluding words, caused by shock or amazement? All there was to it? Frank Alexander James, alias Buck Woods, tossed aside the tragic affair with an airy wave of his hand. His brother Jesse seemed flabbergasted but, for once, made no comment.

"Cole, hardened to the horrors of war, shook his head in unbelief, stared at Frank and said, 'Buck, you must have been out of your mind.'

"Frank James, the first of the three men to enter the bank and the last of the same three to come out, admitted firing one of the two shots heard exploding, seemingly simultaneously in the bank after Pitts and Bob came out. Frank also admitted, even stressed the fact, Mr. Heywood was the only one to offer resistance. No one entered the bank after the three; only Pitts and Bob left before the shooting. Frank James was the only person to come out after the two shots were fired inside the bank—heard outside by Jesse James, Charley Pitts and Cole, Bob and Jim Younger. (I do not vouch for the citizens.)

"Whether my feeling toward Jesse James has been all these, I will say this. At no time was he in the bank. He had no part in the killing of Mr. Heywood, other than like we three Youngers, accessory by being there. Stiles had safely eliminated himself during the uproar, when he left the bridge. Miller was dead in the street. He had paid dearly for his small role in the tragic drama. He had in reality closed the door for Atroper.

"Frank asked Jesse how it happened that he, Frank, was riding the buckskin instead of the bay? Jesse explained that the bay was rearing and plunging at the tie rack and he, Jesse, was afraid *the* bay would break away as Bob's had done and leave Frank afoot. The buckskin being more manageable, he made the change to quiet the bay. I must concede Jesse had a soothing way with horses. He was never brutal nor did he use a harsh bit or spurs, which pleased me of course. In the development of later statements regarding the rider of the buckskin, as he, Frank, rode out of North-field, his motive for so doing was and still is debatable.

"A cold drizzle had set in. Pitts asked if he could do anything for Cole, Bob or me. I said yes, that in the bed rolls on Bob's mount was Miller's raincoat and also one in my roll, and we would like his too, offering Pitts his heavy top coat, which Charley refused saying his seaman's reefer was waterproof and warm, adding 'Besides, you fellows got to keep them shot up laces dry. I'm as healthy as one of Paw's old Missouri mules.' Frank or Jesse made no offer of assistance, showed no seeming interest just watched in silence as Pitts tried and did make us more comfortable.

"Cole said we should be moving out. It would soon be dark, the rain and muddy roads would slow us down. Jesse became sarcastic saying, 'Bob will slow us down more than the roads. Why don't we shoot him, put him out of his misery or swap nags with Charley. We five can ride out, Bob can take his time.' Twenty years have passed since I heard Jesse James' demonic suggestion. It still seems as though I heard his shocking remark in a bad dream.

"Cole and I drew our revolvers, but Bob called out, 'No Bud. You remember Jesse gave his word in K.C. There would be no shooting. No killing. I'd like to see if he is man enough to keep his word. I know he can't outdraw you, but does he?' Pitts had drawn his revolver also, saying as he turned toward Jesse, 'Boys, I'll take care of this pole cat for you, I didn't promise not to shoot anybody.' Again it was Bob who called out, 'No, Charley. Let it ride.'

"For the first time in the seventeen days Jesse, Stiles, Miller and I had been together, Jesse revealed his true character, ruthless and vindictive, an entirely different person than he had been on the ride north. I was amazed that any sane man was capable of such a complete lack of concern for our welfare, our injuries and safety, in venting his defeat and wrath at Frank's stupidity, on we three Youngers, in no way to blame that his scheme, his dream bubble, had burst.

"Still in shocked amazement, we four, Cole, Pitts, Bob and I, were brought back to reality quickly, as without a word of warning, Frank turned, faced Jesse, slapped him viciously back and forth across his face twice as he said, 'I ever hear you say a thing like that again, I'll forget you are my brother and treat you like I would a mad dog. Right now I am not proud of being related to you.'

"Frank too had changed suddenly. One moment his attitude expressed utter indifference to the entire situation or to our injuries or future, shifting abruptly to violent fury as the fickle pendulum of time, swinging far in the opposite direction changes life from one extreme to another. Or did Frank merely assume the pose to further befuddle his goggle-eyed gallery? If that were his intention, Frank James succeeded admirably in deceiving all of us, including his brother Jesse, who, stunned for a moment by Frank's unexpected blows, surprisingly said nothing, made no rash move but his emotions and resentment showed plainly in his eyes as he stared in unbelief at Frank. Was he on the verge of having one of his tantrums? I wonder."

The operative word in this description of Jesse's remarks might be that he became "sarcastic." It seems Jesse was making an ill-timed, callous joke. Even if he had been thinking such a thought, he would surely know that the Youngers wouldn't take kindly to such a brutal suggestion, whether or not it was a "joke."

Cole Younger, to his friend Harry Hoffman, on his deathbed in 1916, would dispute that nothing of the kind had been issued from Jesse's mouth, saying "No, Jesse James, nor any person, ever made that request or suggestion." He said that the last night the group had all been together, Frank and Jesse were able to secure two more fresh horses and that Jesse suggested that Cole and Bob take the horses and ride out while the others continued on foot. Cole declined, telling Jesse and Frank to take the horses and go. He went on to add, "Their acts and treatment of us were honorable and loyal."

We will never know whether Jim took Jesse's bad joke too literally or Cole revised what had occurred, as he was wont to do.

"I am sure it was Cole's intention, as he broke the awkward tension, not only to avert another crisis but also to update Jesse on the pertinent event relating to the purchasing of the mount he, Jesse, was about to ride, perhaps declare as Frank's property," Jim continued.

"Speaking quietly yet positively, Cole made it quite plain to Frank he and Jesse should ride fast and far from us, adding 'you will of course enlighten your brother Jesse as to who paid for the animal he now rides. Also mention as to who it was paid for the one killed and the one that broke from the hitch rack, both back in town. My dapple here, and the one Pitts says he is deeply grateful for, makes five animals in all. Can you, if questioned, prove legal ownership to any one, or all?'

"Frank, gesturing aimlessly with his left hand said, 'I can't pay you now, Bud. I'm broke and Dingus and me just can't ride double on that buckskin.' Cole grinned. 'Charley and I did all right for a spell. But don't put yourself

out on our account. We'll make out.' Cole spoke softly, with
no show of anger, but Frank knew he was not to be fooled
with.

"Frank, shrugging his shoulders (back to the old
who-gives-a-hoot attitude) turned, walked to where
the buckskin was cropping grass, gathering up the reins.
Frank led the horse back to where Cole leaned against
a tree. 'Bud,' Frank said. 'I'll sure keep in touch and you
can depend on it. I'll send the money for the horses.'
Cole grunted, 'I'm from Missouri too, remember?' Then
added, 'don't bother.'"

Cole's allusion to being from Missouri was a reference to the
popular motto that Missouri was the "Show Me" state; that people
in Missouri didn't take things on face value.

"Before Frank could mount and without holstering my
.44, I rode closer to Jesse but spoke directly to Frank,"
Jim writes. "'After the enlightening disclosure of facts
just mentioned by Bud, as your brother to explain to you
the ownership of two "nags"—not mine and used by two
members of his party.

"'Bill Stiles doubtless believed, quite wisely, distance
from Northfield would lend enchantment to his future well
being, the more remote the distance, the more favorable
were his chances of survival and extending his life span, So
he resorted to French leave with one hundred and forty-
five dollars of horseflesh and gear belonging to me.' I was
wound up and went on talking.

"'The other nag was ridden by Clell Miller until his
recent death. A few moments ago, as you will recall, your

brother Jesse James suggested mayhem as a means of illegally acquiring ownership of that particular horse and gear, thereby adding a second horse thief to his motley crew of half-wits.'

"Jesse broke in, saying 'you can't say I didn't pay you for the buckskin.' I cut him short. 'Yes,' I agreed, 'You paid for your mount only. I did not have to replace your saddle and blanket, as I did the other two, so warm they would have caused sores on the horses' backs.'"

"'You seem to have a convenient lapse of memory,' I spoke to Jesse. 'As at that time of payment, you assured me your brother Frank would promptly reimburse me for the two mounts and gear immediately upon meeting him and his party today. As yet he has not done so.'"

"'Clell Miller's tragic death in no way alters the fact that I still own the horse he so recently rode, but more to be considered and remembered is my brother Bob, will be up on that same horse, alive when we ride away from here. Any other idea to the contrary, just isn't a healthy one.'"

"In all my long outburst, Frank made no attempt to interrupt. He may have wanted to argue the matter, if so he gave no indication, perhaps sensing, as I declared myself, the James boys in no way intimidated or over-awed me. His now familiar gesture of his hands, as he toes the buckskins stirrup, was the only outward sign of his reaction. Settling in the hull, without looking at me, his comment was brief. 'Like I told Bud. I'll keep in touch.' My not so brilliant reply was, 'Like Bud said, I'm from Missouri too. Don't bother.'"

This was an unusual outburst for the normally quiet Jim. It seems that the stress and horrors of the previous weeks had finally taken their toll.

"No one spoke," says Jim. "As Frank and Jesse turned to ride off, Frank asked, 'You siding us, Charley?' Pitts answered emphatically, 'No sir. I sure ain't. I might have to stomp me a snake if I ride with you fellows. Or my nag might be swiped, no telling. I might wake up some morning and find my throat slit.' Then stepping closer to Frank he said, 'Buck, here's the six bits I didn't spend. You will maybe need it. Now I only owe you a dollar. I'll pay you some day, if I keep in touch.'

"Frank accepted the coins in unabashed silence. Without further urging, or word of farewell, their mounts responding to a slight lift of bridle reins, Frank and Jesse James rode away.

"No regrets were winced at their going. Perhaps Pitts, Cole and Bob were of my opinion, that in leaving us, the Messers. James had unknowingly relieved a particular tension their attitude had aroused deep within each of us.

"Bob broke the depressive spell. Suffering and upset as we three Youngers were, he tried to clown. Grinning impishly at me as I dismounted so Pitts could loosen Black Beauty's cinch, Bob said, 'Methinks my brother Jim gave the lately departed, unlamented Dingus and Buck James duo quite a verbal trouncing. When our Jim is riled, he's wild. Don't ever get caught with your foot in your mouth around him. He could make you swallow it.' Cole and Pitts had a hearty laugh at my expense, though it did not lessen our grave predicament.

"Pitts asked if we had extra shirts enough. He could make more bandages. Cole and I did have. Charley then more than proved his concern for us in attending our wounds. I had put a fair sized tin of salve in each of the four saddlebags at Albert Lea in case a mount developed back sores. Pitts used it generously on each of us saying, 'It sure can't do any harm, might relieve you some.' It did temporarily. Cole had a can of balsam oil, using both as Pitts did; the combined odor was rather disruptive to our olfactory nerves.

"I have never known where Frank and Jesse James went, or how they avoided capture after they left us, with the buckskin figuring so prominently in the Northfield affair.

"They may have acquired fresh mounts through a trade in. However, with that supposition, the buckskin might have had to be explained unless the 'trade' was a steal (all my own expressed opinions)."

Jim's account ends here. Frank and Jesse followed the Blue Earth River. In forty-eight hours, they had crossed the Minnesota border into South Dakota. Stealing horses along the way, they rode through Sioux Falls to continue their retreat and avoid any attempts of a posse to capture them.

The Youngers had a rougher time. Near Linden, below the Crystal Road, they left their camp abruptly when they heard nearby horses. A posse found some of their possessions: a ripped, backless shirt, a shirt with the initials G. S. O., a blood-soaked handkerchief, a blue gossamer coat, a brown linen duster, two leather bridles, and a piece of carpet. Bob would later say that the two coats were his.

The ragged group followed the road along Lake Linden where they encountered a young man milking cows named Oscar Sorbel. They asked if they might buy some bread. Oscar was suspicious that the men were the Northfield bank robbers and finally convinced his father of his theory. He rode into nearby Madelia and informed Sheriff James Glispen who immediately formed a posse and rode in the direction Sorbel claimed to have seen the men.

As the Youngers and Charlie attempted to elude the posse by first hiding in the boggy Hanska Slough, a gunfight erupted. The Youngers luck ran out in the wooded area just above the Watawon River. Upon realizing that they were surrounded and that things were not likely to go their way this time, Charlie suggested to Cole that they surrender. Cole responded, "Charlie, this is where Cole Younger dies." The ever-loyal Charley Pitts nodded. "All right, Captain, I can die as game as you can. Let's get it done." Those would be Charlie's last words. In the hail of gunfire that followed he fell dead, riddled with bullets.

Cole was shot several times, including a bullet that hit his face and lodged over his right eye. Jim fared no better. Along with his four other wounds, he was the recipient of a rifle ball that hit him in the jaw, taking out several of his teeth and lodging in his mouth. Bob looked at the damage done to his brothers and his friend Charlie and yelled at the posse to stop their firing. Cole started to protest but Bob called out, "I surrender. They're all down but me." As Glispin ordered the firing to halt, Bob staggered up the bank holding a handkerchief in his raised left hand. A shot came from the group watching him and Bob was struck in the chest. As Bob fell to the ground, he called weakly, "Somebody shot me while I was surrendering!" The angry Glispin told his men that he would personally shoot the next man who fired.

As the posse proceeded to advance on the three Youngers, Cole offered to fight them hand to hand. Bob looked at his defeated warrior brother and told him, "Cole, it's over. Give it up or they will hang us for sure."

Jesse James' crazy, contested idea to ride so far out of the gang's known area to rob the bank of a people he underestimated was finally at an end.

CHAPTER 9

A Tragic New Life

Cole, Jim, and Bob were helped up the bank and loaded into a wagon. All three were in bad shape. Jim leaned his profusely bleeding face over the side. At one point along the way to the nearby town of Madelia, the family of George Thompson passed by in a buggy. Cole and Charlie had visited Thompson's store in St. James and exchanged friendly conversation with Thompson. Mrs. Thompson now gave Jim a handkerchief to hold over his chin.

The Youngers were taken to the Flanders Hotel, owned by another man Cole and Charlie had encountered, Colonel Thomas Vought. Vought had been in the posse. When Cole saw him he cordially called him "landlord." The three brothers were taken to beds on the second floor of the hotel. Cole and Jim were placed in one bed and Bob was taken to another bed at the opposite end of the hall. Two doctors named Overholt and Cooley were called in to examine their wounds.

The three outlaws were such a pathetic sight that the townspeople couldn't help but feel some sympathy for them. Fresh clothing was donated to make them more comfortable. That didn't mean they were not treated as dangerous criminals. A strong guard was placed in and around the hotel less any of the Youngers' friends or admirers got it into their heads to rescue them. In the meantime, crowds in the hundreds gathered outside. (Charlie Pitts' body was placed in the small Madelia jail with his fatal chest wound exposed while sightseers were allowed to pass by to view the dead outlaw.)

It had been previously agreed by the Youngers that if they were to be captured, the names of themselves or others involved in the robbery would not be revealed. By the time the Youngers were in the hands of the law, however, St. Louis Police Chief James McDonough had already identified the bodies of Clell Miller and Bill Stiles with the help of the Pinkertons. When Cole and Bob were questioned, they freely admitted their identities. Jim was unable to speak because of the severity of his wound. Before the Youngers and Jameses were determined to likely be the robbers, some newspapers suggested that Texas outlaw Cal Carter was behind the attack on the bank. Word now went up that the third man, in fact Jim Younger, was the infamous Carter. Another rumor about Jim arose. The rumor was spread that it was Jim, not Bob, who had been shot by a man named Willis Bundy upon surrender as he lay helplessly on the ground.

They were relieved of the few possessions they had left. Cole said that they had given their money, watches, and rings to their escaping comrades. Cole and Bob had five dollars in their billfolds. Jim had $150. He didn't trust the Jameses and kept his money.

The men were allowed to sleep that night, something that they hadn't been able to do for quite some time in the bush. Jim likely didn't receive much rest as he continued to bleed from his mouth wound and his wound was repeatedly cauterized.

In the morning, Cole and Bob were ready to talk. Jim still remained silent but listened in awe as Cole told his life story with great relish. Both Cole and Bob expressed gratitude to their captors; they had expected to be immediately hanged. When asked to name his accomplices, Cole clearly stated, "Stay by your friends even if Heaven falls." That was to be the end of that.

The men were to be transferred to the Northfield county seat of Faribault but Jim's injury was still not under control and for the time being, his doctors thought better of that idea. They gave him another day but the next day they were all placed onboard the St. Paul and Sioux City Railroad. Hundreds of people gathered to meet the train and view the outlaws.

The Youngers were taken to the small Faribault Jail and placed in separate cells measuring 7' high and 3½' wide. The small space was a hardship on the 6'2"Bob, but Jim was still in too much pain to care. Cole somehow talked himself out of his cell and was allowed to sit outside the area on a cot near the door. Then the circus began. By September 26, over 4,000 people were allowed in to walk past the cells and "view" the outlaws. Of course, the newspapers had a field day. Cole regaled them with his stories of how they had been driven to commit the crime because of all the devastating incidents that occurred to them during the war and after. But these Yankees weren't buying it. The newspaper tore him to shreds. Even his brothers were disgusted with the obvious play for sympathy. Bob gained the respect of the press by owning his deeds and expressing regret. Jim said little; it hurt to talk and he didn't care to share his thoughts anyway.

Officer James McDonough out of St. Louis and C. B. Hunn of the United States Express Company, along with identifications from Hobbs Kerry, who had participated with the Gang in the robbery of a train in Otterville, Missouri, just previous to the trip to Northfield, were able to identify Charlie Pitts, Cole Younger, and Bob Younger. Since no identification of the fourth man—Jim, who had not participated in the Otterville robbery—was forthcoming, Jim continued to be identified as Cal Carter. Although Jim shook his head that no, he wasn't Cal Carter and Cole and Bob told the authorities that he was their brother, McDonough continued to believe Jim was Cal Carter. Cole offered to bet McDonough $500 that he was wrong.

The Surgeon General of Minnesota was called in to examine Jim's wound. He found that the bullet that had entered Jim's jaw was still embedded in front of his left ear and pressing lightly against his brain. Jim continued to suffer acute pain.

Mayor Ames of Northfield tried to accuse Cole of firing the bullet that had killed Nicholas Gustavson, even though the coroner's jury had already determined that it was a stray bullet fired by an "unknown party" that had caused the man's death.

John Merriam, the man who had been humiliated at Gad's Hill came to call. Cole recognized him and asked if they had met before. But when Merriam accused Cole of being one of the Gad's Hill robbers, Cole denied it.

The following day, the three Youngers were photographed in their cells. Jim was seriously depressed and in pain; he lay on his cot staring at the ceiling.

On October 5, the boys received a visit from their sister Retta, in the company of their brother-in-law, Dick Hall. Retta broke down when she saw Jim and at last McDonough accepted that "Cal Carter" was indeed Jim Younger.

Jim, Cole, and Bob remained in the Faribault jail for over a month. Thomas Rutledge was eventually chosen as their attorney. On November 9, they met again with Retta and Hall to decide what course of action they should take when the charges were declared.

On November 18, Cole, Jim, and Bob were escorted into a packed courtroom, their faces stoic as people around them jeered. They were charged with accessory to the murder of Joseph Heywood, attacking A. E. Bunker with intent to do bodily harm and the robbery of the First National Bank of Northfield. Additionally, Cole, as principal, and Jim and Bob as accessories, were charged with the murder of Nicholas Gustavson.

Each man was called to stand before the judge and each declared himself guilty. Their attorney had told them earlier that if they pled guilty, they would not be hung. They were asked individually if they had any response to the charges, and each one replied no. At that point, Judge Samuel Lord pronounced that Coleman, James, and Robert Younger were to be confined to the state prison to the end of their natural lives. Rutledge told them if they behaved themselves while behind bars, they would likely be eligible for parole in ten years.

On November 20, the Youngers boarded a train bound for St. Paul. There they were transferred to a wagon that would take them to the prison in Stillwater. Along the way, a curious thing happened. There were the usual crowds, come to see the now-famous outlaws, but many in the crowd yelled their support and encouragement to the men. That was appreciated but nothing could relieve the gloom of the waiting walls of the prison where the three Missouri boys would spend a very long time.

CHAPTER 10
Defeat and Confusion

As he entered Stillwater Penitentiary, Jim lost his personal identity when he became Prisoner #700. After he was searched and bathed, he was given the black and white striped uniform of a third-grade prisoner. His body parts were measured according to the Bertillon System, and he was led to a 5'×7' cell, which contained a Bible, two cups, a mirror, a spoon, two towels, soap, a comb, a water jar, a bed, and linen. After all the crowds and gawkers he'd been exposed to, he likely found the solitude to be a relief. He and his brothers were assigned the task of making tubs and bucket, working in the basement. They were not allowed to speak to one another.

After a short time, the Warden realized that these men were not his average prisoner. He elevated them to second-grade and their privileges expanded to include the ability to write two letters a month, see visitors once a month, eat in a dining room instead of their cells, and visit with one another once a month. Jim and Cole were assigned to work in the thresher factory, where Jim made belts.

The greatest privilege Jim would receive was that now he could take advantage of the prison library and read to his heart's content. Yet even that was hard for him as he suffered from severe headaches as a result of his wound. His life was made even more difficult, as he would never again be able to eat solid food and was forced to take his meals through a straw.

Robberies by Jesse James continued along with the drama of his new gang. Jesse became rightfully paranoid about not being able to trust his "friends" and his actions reflected that. The culmination of an adult life lived outside the law and being continuously hunted resulted in Jesse allowing himself to be murdered by his most recent recruit, Bob Ford, on April 3, 1882. He had simply had enough. Frank James would surrender himself later that year but remarkably be found innocent of all crimes.

The three Youngers never said what they thought about Jesse's death. Cole needed proof and asked his sister Retta to check the body in St. Joseph to confirm that it was indeed Jesse. It was. (Jesse obviously was familiar to various members of the Younger family prior to Northfield.) Jim no doubt was relieved that Jesse James was out of his life and that of his brother Bob. Jim's prison life continued, the daily routine something of a comfort to him.

On January 8, 1884, someone set fire to the prison's woodworking shop and two storage buildings. Two weeks later, the entire prison erupted into flames. Head Guard George F. Dodd, who had become friendly with the Youngers, was in charge of evacuating the prisoners. He had his hands full. As he rushed past Cole, Cole asked if there was anything he could do to help. Dodd needed to evacuate the women prisoners and knew he couldn't do it without assistance. To Cole's astonishment, he was given a revolver, Bob an iron bar, and Jim an axe. They were told to escort the women to safety. After this was accomplished, they surrendered their weapons. No attempt to run from the prison was attempted. The Youngers had once again demonstrated that they were not the usual prisoner.

Cole, Jim, and Bob were temporarily housed in the Washington County jail for a month while the prison was repaired. When they returned to the Stillwater Penitentiary, completing their ninth year of incarceration, Bob was put to work binding books, Cole became one of the librarians, and Jim was put in charge of the mail. Jim enjoyed his work but when Cole was appointed a hospital trustee, Jim became head librarian. He was quite happy with this assignment and read everything he could get his hands on. He especially liked current events and began to write about the subjects that interested him.

After serving the tenth year of their incarceration, talk of parole began. It was not uncommon for those with life sentences to be considered for parole after this time if their prison records were clean, which those of the three brothers were. The Youngers' aunt, Frances Twyman, sister of their mother (who had died on June 6, 1870) decided that she would become actively involved in her nephews' parole drive. She was the very much respected wife of a prominent doctor and had many influential friends. Former Confederate soldier Warren Bronaugh also decided to become involved, possibly at the secret request of Frank James. And the woman who would become the Youngers' staunchest advocate, Cora Lee McNeil Deming, came aboard.

"Mama had corresponded with Cole and Jim and with their sister Rhetta Rawlins (nee Younger) of Dallas, Texas during the Younger imprisonment," wrote Deedee Deane. "It was during a visit to Cole and Jim that W.C. Bronaugh of Kansas City, Mo.—at that time I think he was a feature writer on the KC Star—and he, Bronaugh, asked what was there he could do to help the Younger cause. Cole told him of Cora Lee—saying, in effect, 'If she will come north, she can do more than any other dozen people can do for us.' Where Cora Lee found the courage to face the hostile north, a stranger in an antagonistic, uncharitable state, only she knew. She did go north, she did work hard for what she believed in. Not one cent was ever contributed to her expenses in living, traveling the many miles she did, or to the support of her three growing children. She used her own money entirely. Nor did she ever receive any remuneration from the published book Mizzoura."

To nourish their creative sides, Jim and Cole became interested in woodworking. They made several pieces of sculpture that they gave to some of their visitors. Cole specialized in walking canes while Jim made boxes and picture frames.

The parole campaign continued, with letters to prominent state officials as well as meetings between those who sought the Youngers parole and those who might have an influence to make that happen. And there were many who believed the Youngers should be set free, after serving their ten years debt to society. Even Missouri Governor Thomas Crittenden, the man who hired Bob Ford to murder Jesse James, believed that the Youngers should now be set free. Another surprise advocate was Minnesota Governor William R. Marshall. Yet there was turmoil in the Minnesota government and paroling the Youngers was not number one on their list of priorities.

As Jim continued to read of national policies and opinions, he grew increasingly bitter. He felt others had long unduly influenced him, although his actions were his own. He began to voice his own strong opinions when he was with his family and friends. He began to write witty and astute illustrated essays, which he shared with his brothers. They encouraged Jim to share them with the prison population, as they felt not only did Jim have a wonderful ability to articulate his point of view but that he also had a strong wit that would be appreciated. Jim said he didn't care to share his personal opinions with others but rather liked the idea of a prison newspaper. He and Cole raised $200 from other prisoners for the venture, and an inmate named Lew Schoonmaker was appointed editor of the newspaper they titled *The Prison Mirror*. The nature of the paper is evident in the newspaper's description of Cole Younger: "Cole Younger, our genial [former] prison librarian, has received new honors at the hands of the *Mirror* by being appointed to the honorable position of 'printer's devil', in which he will in the future keep flies off the gifts of 'wedding cake', and other editorial favors of like nature which may find lodgment in our inner sanctorum." *The Prison Mirror* was a great success and to this day has a reputation as the oldest, most continuously published prison newsletter in the United States.

While Jim and his brothers were enjoying the written word and cautiously looking forward to success with their parole, all hell was breaking loose in that endeavor. John Newman Edwards drafted a petition of parole which was signed by twenty-eight of the members of the General Assembly of Missouri and sent to the new Governor of Minnesota, William R. Merriam.

The parole campaign gained momentum. Especially noteworthy was the addition of Minnesota's first governor, Henry H. Sibley who came onboard as an ally.

Sibley wrote, "Minnesota has shown her power to punish malefactors, let her now manifest her magnanimity, by opening the prison doors to the men who have so long suffered for a violation of her laws, and bid them 'go and sin no more'." Those involved waited to see how the new Governor would react.

Bob Younger had become good friends with Deputy Warden Jacob Westby. The two men often conversed and sometimes Bob would share his thoughts. In the spring of 1883, Westby began to notice that Bob was pale and often very tired. When he asked him about it, Bob said that he had been fighting off lung congestion ever since he had received the chest wound on the day of his capture. Westby encouraged Bob to consult with the prison doctor but Bob shook off the suggestion. When Westby finally insisted the doctor see him, Bob was diagnosed with phthisis, also known as pulmonary tuberculosis. When Bob was told he didn't have much longer to live, the thirty-four-year-old man reacted calmly, having figured that out for himself. Bob told his brothers of his prognosis but asked them not to discuss it in his presence. He would continue with the efforts for parole, with hope that he might be able to return to Missouri and die there.

The diligent efforts of their friends continued. Former Union Army Colonel E. F. Rogers, Warren "Wal" Bronaugh, and Confederate Officer Stephen Reagan canvassed the Minnesota citizenry and obtained 163 letters that agreed that the Youngers had served enough time and should be set free. The parole activists were able to enlist more esteemed elected officials to lend their names to the campaign, including even members of the posse who had captured the Youngers all those years ago.

It was time to bring their extended effort to the one man who could make their great hope a reality: current Minnesota Governor William R. Merriam.

Merriam barely looked at the extensive documents and letters. Brushing them aside he curtly responded: "I cannot pardon these men. My duty to the state and my personal prejudice against them make it impossible."

Everyone was flabbergasted.

It was only after nearly a hundred years later that the facts behind Merriam's cold decision were revealed. John L. Merriam, the man who had been humiliated at the hands of the Gad's Hill train robbers, was the father of William R. Merriam. Without revealing his reason, Governor Merriam was at last getting his family's revenge for the act.

The devastated group decided that the parole drive would somehow continue and that eventually Merriam could be persuaded to change his mind. The focus became Bob's desire to die in his home state. Marshall and Bronaugh returned to Merriam with that request. Merriam was as uncompromising as he was the previous time: "I would not pardon the Youngers even if Mrs. Heywood [who had died since her husband's murder] should come to life again and make the request."

Wal Bronaugh wrote: "Merriam was as merciless as an avenging Nemesis. Every resource at our command had been exhausted to mollify him."

The message was clear as Merriam made no excuses when he then chose to parole another prisoner with a life sentence. That prisoner had been convicted of murdering his wife, stuffing her body under the floor, and holding a party in their home over her dead body the evening of her murder.

Bob's time was running out and his brothers bore the weight of his foolish decision to ride with Jesse James in 1876. They had forgiven him years ago, but it was still a painful burden for Bob to bear. Retta Younger traveled once again to Minnesota. At 6:00 p.m. on September 16, 1889, Bob asked his brothers, sister, and Deputy Warden Westby to stay with him in his hospital room. While listening to a birdcall outside his window, Bob reminded Cole of the birds back home in Missouri. He asked that his brothers raise him so that he might see the sky again and said that when he died, he thought his soul might rest a moment on the hill outside the window. At 10:30 p.m., Bob Younger closed his eyes and died. It was only his body that was returned to Missouri, to be laid to rest next to his mother in Lee's Summit.

With the governor's heart hardened even against letting Bob return to die in Missouri, Jim became morose and even more depressed. He believed that all hope of parole was now at an end.

He sought comfort in his books and his job. Keeping busy helped keep his mind occupied and he asked the warden if, in addition to his job in the library, he could also handle the mail. The warden agreed; he liked Jim and hated to see him so defeated.

John Ryder of the *Kansas City World* visited Jim and Cole. Ryder reported:

Cole had the preferable place as far as light, air and roominess were concerned. Jim's workroom was cramped; but he communed daily, hourly with the illuminated minds of the world, dead or alive. The older, stronger man [Cole} was ever in contact with acute suffering or patient misery, living in the drug store atmosphere, relieved only by the duty of ministering to pain or chiding petulance. The man with the bullets in his body [Jim}, causing many an unseen twinge, found among the bookcases and their contents, work to keep his brooding mind occupied to the point of contentment almost.

Governor Merriam came up for reelection and won two more years in office. Cole asked Bronaugh to continue his efforts for parole but it was really a useless case with Merriam still at the helm.

Ben West, from Harrisonville, visited Cole and Jim and his observation of Jim's state of mind was not favorable either:

Jim seems discouraged and has evidently given up hope. He plainly shows the effects of his wounds and close confinement. Large rings under his eyes and his nervous movements show him to be in bad physical condition.

It was clear that Jim needed help. Cole knew just the person to turn to: Cora Lee McNeil.

Cora Lee had married since Jim had been in prison. She and her husband, E. J. Deming, had three children but Deming had died and now Cora Lee was a widow. She visited Jim and Cole now on a regular basis, having relocated to the area. Cora Lee's daughter Deedee remembered visiting "The Boys" at Stillwater when she was a young girl.

I wrote {to a Younger relative] of my visits with mama to Stillwater. The waiting room business—guards—boys coming to the waiting room—guards announcing "times up," all a surprise to me. We did not go thru that routine ever. Mama of course always stopped in the office and registered, sometimes chatted with Warden Wolfer, then went directly to the library where Jim was, and Cole joined us when he was off duty from the hospital. No doubt but that Mama seldom, if ever, took advantage of the usual visiting hours. On the other hand, the Warden and guards were aware that she was working for the Boys release. They liked the Boys, felt that they served their time well for their part in the raid, so did not object to the time Mama spent with the Boys.

James H. Younger was fifty when I first saw him in 1898. He was not as heavy as Cole yet was well built, was five foot ten inches tall, weight 180–190 lbs. Eyes dark blue, his hair was a very dark auburn, almost brown. Spoke with a soft Southern drawl, deep sense of humor. Loved children, animals, birds. Played the violin and quite well. Talking was difficult. Was forced to wear a mustache because of ugly wound in mouth, part of palate had been shot away. Took his meals in his cell because the mouth wound made eating difficult. He never granted an interview to a stranger. Was very much interested in "New Thought" if originated by P. Quimby. Also liked Blavatsay' teachings.

Phineas Quimby was the founder of New Thought, a movement blending Christianity and Metaphysics. Helena Blavatsky was a Russian occultist and philosopher who co-founded the esoteric religion of Theosophy, which claimed God could be known through direct intuition. Jim was very interested in philosophy and religion.

A new Governor had been elected in 1893 but Knute Nelson served only one term and hardly had time to devote to a parole drive for the Youngers. It's doubtful that he was ever even approached. When Nelson left the office of Governor to serve in the US Senate, Lieutenant Governor David M. Clough became governor.

Cora Lee vowed to do all she could for the parole movement and set about contacting as many influential people as she was able.

The current General Assembly of Missouri signed the Edwards petition and former Minnesota governors Andrew McGill and William Marshall continued to be supportive. Jim's former teacher Stephen Elkins was now a US Senator representing West Virginia. He signed on to help Cora Lee and Wal Bronaugh.

In October 1896, Bronaugh, current Stillwater Warden Henry Wolfer, the Youngers' nephew Harry Jones (by then an attorney), State Auditor R. C. Dunn, and State Senator James O'Brian met with Governor Clough in his office to present the Youngers' case. But Clough was on the fence and couldn't make up his mind. He asked the men to obtain another petition and submit it to the newly formed Board of Pardons.

It wasn't difficult to get another signed petition, along with another slew of support by impressive individuals, thanks to Cora Lee and Bronaugh. Yet this time, another wrinkle had to be met. The board demanded that if Cole and Jim wanted them to consider their parole, they must answer three questions: Was Frank James in the bank? Who was the last person who left the bank? And who was the man on the buckskin horse? The ever-faithful Cole and Jim, even though their very liberty was at stake, weren't prepared to answer those questions. The parole was denied.

The people of Northfield and the surrounding area were pleased and smug editorials abounded in the newspapers. Jim was so dismayed about the verdict that he swore to never talk to the press again. He was through with active participation in a parole drive that continued to end up without positive results. He would continue to lose himself in his intellectual pursuits.

Dr. Morrill Withrow, the doctor with whom Cole was working at the time, later wrote of Jim:

Jim . . . had the most astounding fund of knowledge that I ever knew in one person . . . he also possessed a most retentive memory and could give the most intimate details of any and all historic events. He once gave a most lucid description of the debates over the adoption of the Constitution, and of every major piece of legislation that had been adopted since the beginning of the history of our country. I used to attempt to dig up some question to ask him to see if it were not possible to puzzle him but I never succeeded in finding one, no matter how abstruse, to which he did not have a ready, offhand explanation.

Cora Lee was pleased that Jim hadn't given up his interests but she continued to work to take actions that might result in his pursuing those interests outside of Stillwater Prison.

CHAPTER 11
A Twist

THE NEXT DEVELOPMENT IN JIM'S STORY CONTAINS TWO EXTREMELY interesting disclosures from Deedee, who refers to her mother as Miss McNeil, instead of Mrs. Deming.

Through the Youngers, Cora Lee McNeil met the Edw. J. Schurmeiers of St. Paul, Minn., close friends of the "boys," on one of her Sunday visits to Stillwater. They too were greatly interested in securing the release of the Youngers.

Mrs. Schurmeier asked if Miss McNeil would consider a dinner invitation for the following week, after which she could meet a number of other friends also interested in the Younger cause and explain her objective and what she hoped to accomplish, seemingly in the face of a still hostile and unforgiving state. Miss McNeil accepted.

Among the after dinner guests was Miss Alix Muller, a St. Paul newspaper feature writer.

Upon learning Miss McNeil was a member of both the United Press and Associated Press, Miss Muller asked if she, Miss McNeil, was on "special assignment." Miss McNeil replied, "Yes, in a way."

Miss McNeil began her explanation of her connection with the Younger case, dating from the time of Capt. Steve

Regan's call on her, at Cole's request in 1896, at her home in Kansas City, Mo.

She voiced the hope that with the help of friends she could overcome the opposition, encountered already at some of her lectures throughout the seemingly unfriendly State of Minn. toward the Youngers in their efforts of freedom.

Miss McNeil suggested to those present who wished to help could do so by writing or talking to friends, legislators, pastors, business associates, urging them to interest others in the cause to which she had dedicated herself.

Miss McNeil also made it quite clear she would not solicit or accept funds; any financial contributions made or suggested be addressed directly to the Youngers. She was financing her own efforts and would continue to do so.

Miss Muller immediately thrust herself into the case, saying, "You can count on my support. They will make bully copy for my column."

Before Miss McNeil could reply, Miss Muller continued, "The next time you visit them, the Youngers, I'll go with you. You simply must introduce me to them. They sound so fascinating. Outlaws always do, don't you think?"

Coming so flippantly, even inanely, on a first meeting, astonished Miss McN especially as it came from a newspaper writer. She asked Miss Muller if she had met the men she referred to as "outlaws"? She, Miss M. replied with a shrug, "There are so many really important people to interview in the Twin Cities. I have no time to make prison calls."

Once in awhile Miss McNeil's gentleness in speech was edged with little sarcastic barbs—not often, however, sometimes bordering on the intentionally naïve. It was so as she again asked Miss Muller, "Why then this sudden decision to meet the Youngers? For over twenty years they have been front page news, the target for all the writers of the sensational yellow journals and dime novels in the world, yet you have never set them up under your by-line?"

Miss Muller admitted she knew nothing of the merits of the case, as the men she so glibly called "outlaws," expressing no interest or concern other than material for her articles, and remarking "I'll run over and interview them the first chance I get."

Alix J. Muller was born in St. Paul, Minnesota, the daughter of John. R. Muller. She moved to Grand Rapids, Michigan, with her father and sister when she was a young girl, allegedly because she suffered from consumption. Apparently recovering, she attended college and became a writer. Returning to St. Paul in 1899, she compiled a history of the St. Paul fire and police departments. By 1900, she was working as a freelance writer for several newspapers, in and out of Minnesota. It was at this time she met Cora Lee McNeil.

"Later in the evening, Miss Muller, extending a card to Miss McNeil said, 'My telephone number. Call me up the next time you go to Stillwater,'" continues Deedee. "'I'll go along. Save me the bother of introducing myself.'

'Ignoring the card, Miss McNeil said, 'You overestimate my ability, Miss Muller. Neither the prison officials or the Youngers have authorized me to sponsor a guest on my pass. You apply thru the regular channels well in advance of your intended visit, giving dates preferred, reason for the interview and your editor's name and press representation.'

If the Youngers and the warden approved, she would in due time receive a pass which was essential at all times, especially so for the first time visitor.

"Miss Muller assured Miss McNeil that her press card and her powers of persuasion were sufficient to gain admittance to the prison, regardless to whether the Youngers liked it or not, any day or any time, adding 'The warden will introduce me. I presume the Youngers know how to meet people.'

"Miss McNeil readily admitted the Youngers were indeed accustomed to meeting all types of the human race from important dignitaries to the fanatical curious. A personal introduction was not necessary. It was entirely up to them to grant an interview and it was also their privilege to refuse, regardless of how important the visitor might feel she or he to be, even to the run of the mill reporters.

"As to Miss Muller's ability to convince the warden of her importance, Miss McNeil had her mental reservations as to the outcome of that first visit. The ostentatious display of utter disregard of prison regulations could only meet with defeat. Furthermore Miss McNeil told herself, some day a crisis would occur between Miss Muller's intense arrogance as against Cora Lee's own rational mental capacity and calm nature.

"On Miss McNeil's next trip to Stillwater, she saw Miss Muller a few seats ahead of her. Neither made any overture to speak. Arriving at Stillwater, Miss Muller hurried to a waiting for hire carriage, giving the driver the prison as her destination in a loud voice. Ignoring her, the driver, having taken Miss McNeil to the prison other times, touched his hat and waited. Miss McNeil smiled, shook her head, saying, 'It's a lovely day. I shall enjoy the walk along the river.'

"Arriving at the visitor's gate, Miss McNeil saw Miss Muller in what seemed to be a heated one-sided argument with the head guard, who with an obdurate look was telling her her name was not on the visitors' list, nor was she known to him. Furthermore, she was without the warden's pass and no, he would not call the warden.

"Miss McNeil walked through another gate, exchanging pleasantries with the guard, who waved her pass aside saying, 'That's alright, Miss McNeil. We know you. Say hello to the Boys from Pete and me.'

"This bit of by-play burst unkind remarks from Miss Muller directed at Miss McNeil and prison guards in particular. She would take the matter up with her close friend the Governor. Nettled by her attitude, the guard said, 'Madam, here you and the governor would be in the same fix, without a pass, if I did not recognize him. Rules are rules and I am hired to enforce them and I am doing just that.'

"Miss McNeil related the incident to the Boys, asking them to at least see Miss Muller once if she was successful in securing the Warden's pass and she much preferred the incident be forgotten. Impressing the fact upon them that though Miss Muller was a stranger, it was possible she did have influential contacts and every one they could muster was urgently needed in what doubtless would be a terrific struggle for them.

"Cole was quite elated, being as he told Cora Lee, a 'lady's man' he was confident he could impress her with his charm. Jim held a pessimistic view of talking with another newspaper 'sob sister.' They were all alike—wrote nothing but trivia and twaddle. But for Cora Lee's sake, he would see her at least once.

"Trying again, Miss Muller did, thru the proper channels. As Cole expressed it, she bowled Cole over with her assumed charm and her assurance she had unlimited connections in 'high places.' No names or the high places were named at the time, according to Cole.

"Jim insisted there would be nothing published without he and Cole first reading the article(s) and approving. This he also wrote to Miss Muller's editor. Jim learned later that several articles he had never read, Miss Muller had smuggled (Cole's word) to Cole for his approval, which had in turn brought down the wrath of other Twin Cities reporters when they appeared under Miss Muller's 'exclusive' by-line.

"Jim told Miss McNeil he had always been acquiescent to Cole. Mainly he, himself, did not seek the publicity as Cole did, but he had now reached the limit of his endurance and had informed the warden that Miss Muller's interviews with him were to be cancelled. Her frequent visits, inane chatter, her persistent annoying attentions directed to him, were not only undesirable but also interrupted his work.

"Jim further commented to Cora Lee, 'Her articles, as she mistakenly calls them, do us more harm than good. Like all the other dime novel fiction about the Youngers, the fantastic tales she falsely attributes to us are but figments of her own weak mind.'

"Cole waggishly observed to Miss McN, 'I feel like a reincarnated Robin Hood, with all her "robbed the rich to help the poor" tales. Jim is pictured as Friar Tuck, just off a rigid diet and with the passing years has grown sedate, serious and solemn.' All of which Jim did not think at all humorous.

"Resenting the warden's order, Miss Muller was in no way discouraged. Cole had told her their mail was not censored—and Jim was mail clerk. She began writing letters to Jim, often times in the same mail, every day. Sometimes they were so bulky as to require extra postage from Jim. This irked Jim and handing a packet of the unopened letters to Cora Lee, requested that she burn them. 'I opened the first two, he said, and am sorry I did, as they sounded as though composed by a mentally unbalanced mind, pouring out the frustrations of a love sick old woman.' This was Jim's only comment as to the letters.

"Receiving no reply to her letters from Jim, Miss Muller went all out by using special delivery means for Sunday delivery. Jim told the warden the letters invariably had postage due and because of that fact he, Jim, refused further acceptance. The prison office then rejected all such material addressed to him.

"The failure of that maneuver did not seem to discourage Miss Muller. She bombarded Cole with letters insisting he urge Jim to answer her, as she was heartbroken over his continued silence, that he loved her but hesitated to admit it to the world from behind bars, to protect her.

"Cole protested to Cora Lee and Jim that his only motive in writing to Miss Muller was to inquire after so long a time since her mention of influential friends, why nothing had come of her assertions and just when could he expect to meet them. He assured Jim his name was not mentioned by him nor would he carry out Miss Muller's demands.

"Miss Muller's reply was that she only wrote to Cole to arouse Jim's jealousy. Cole showing the letter to Jim and Cora Lee showed his chagrin. Jim for once relished a bit of ribbing he gave Cole, saying to Cora Lee, 'The old man had his ego deflated at long last.'

"The letters to Cole from Miss Muller, thereafter, received the same fate as Jim's, Cole remarking he too could contribute fuel to keep the home fire burning. Cole then requested the warden to revoke Miss Muller's pass. He, like Jim, was disgusted with her lack of propriety and as Jim said, 'They could maybe insult her but neither of them had ever knowingly insulted a female. Nor did they know how to go about it and they hesitated to establish a precedent.'

"The guards refusing Miss Muller's pass on her next visit, she again created a scene. She really would take the matter up with her close friend, Gov. Van Sant. There was sure to be a thorough cleaning out of present officials including guards at Stillwater Prison. The guards ignored her, simply asking her to step aside as other visitors were waiting to enter.

"A *Minneapolis Tribune* reporter, friend of the Boys, told them he was in the Gov.'s office 'copying data' when to quiet Miss Muller's ranting outside the open door, the Gov. had her admitted, interrupting his talk with the 'Trib' reporter.

"Storming into the office, she demanded the Gov. fire the warden's guards and all officials connected with the prison. She had been grossly insulted, also been refused, a member of the Press, admission on business to a public institution. As a taxpayer, she was being ignored. Furthermore, demanding a lifetime pass and the annulling of Miss McNeil's pass. She was a trouble maker, Miss Muller asserted, adding, 'I pay taxes too, remember.'

"The governor, a bachelor, was noted for his short temper toward people who made demands of him and his office. He resented the inane inference of taxpayers in any and all cases. It did not influence him at all, only irritated.

"Cora Lee McNeil was well known to Gov. Van Sant. She had been his only personally escorted guest on several State occasions, openly approving her efforts in behalf of the Youngers in the hostile state of Minnesota.

"A letter from the warden explaining the situation made the Governor quite caustic in his remarks to Miss Muller, which failed utterly to indicate any close friendship or liking for her attitude, saying 'Miss Muller, I would not grant you your silly demands if you were my mother, which thank a thoughtful Providence you are not. Your interview is over. Don't ever presume to request another, here or in Stillwater. Next visitor, please.'

"Jim was elated. Peace had again descended on his little world. Evening chats with other inmates as to books they might enjoy, time spent teaching English or himself a foreign language; Cora Lee's letters and visits cheering him greatly, he was soon back to his normal outlook, regaining a more serene hold on life.

"Miss Muller was not easily discouraged. A few failures in her ambitions did not deter her for long. Soon she devised another way to satisfy her vanity and feed her self-importance.

"The next efforts were directed toward Miss McNeil and was her usual mode of annoyance, letters, which could only be conceived in her own unbalanced mind, without any thought of that the result might be to herself.

"In nearly every letter Miss Muller repeated her charge that Miss McNeil lured Jim from her by promising that Jim and Miss McNeil would marry secretly when he received his parole. There was no explanation as to how they would accomplish that.

"Miss Muller described herself as being Jim's 'Soul Mate.' Explaining his reason for ignoring her letters, she said he was reluctant to openly and freely confess his deep love for her while behind bars, even tho she had assured him many times she was his 'bride in the sight of Heaven' and he had not denied it. It was love at first sight, she claimed.

"In another letter, Miss Muller underscored these words, 'You have caused me and my lover so much heartache, but very soon you will regret it as something will happen to you very soon.'

"Miss McNeil was shocked. She had told no one of the letters as they continued to arrive thru the mail. She reluctantly consulted Judge George Bennett, pointing out for her own peace of mind and perhaps Miss Muller's sanity; the situation could no longer be ignored. The inconsistency of the entire affair reached the limit of her own mental and physical endurance."

Judge George Bennett was an eligible bachelor with a serious interest in the intelligent and self-assured Cora Lee McNeil. Cora Lee had rebuffed his attraction to her, her focus being on Jim Younger. That didn't stop the judge from his continued designs on

Cora Lee; he didn't see how she could possibly be attracted to the old outlaw regardless of the fact that they shared a common background back home in Missouri.

Deedee continues:

Miss McNeil attributed Miss Muller's infatuation for Jim as being self-imposed, sustained mainly by her inability to break through his reserve.

Her emotional passion, which she maintained in the face of his indisputable resistance, resulting in her failure to arouse a responsive chord in Jim, his silence only made her more determined.

Reading the letters, the judge's equanimity was considerably shaken yet being the astute lawyer that he was, he saw further possibilities for the furtherance of his own plans, through the thoughtless and utter disregard of the law and the resulting repercussions by Miss Muller.

Forcing Miss Muller's discontinuous of her harassment of Miss McNeil through intimidation if necessary, suasive power by preference would increase Miss McNeil's, as yet unknown to her, indebtedness to him. It could heighten his prestige with the Boys, at least until the bill was presented, appeal for passage and if any, a rebuttal offered by the state Atty. General.

Or if the Boys were not satisfied entirely, regarding the terms of the pending bill in the event of its passing, they could do nothing. In their desire for freedom, a parole if not full pardon, it would simply be a matter of their accepting the written conditions with Chief Justice Start verbally inserting one article of conduct to which the Youngers must agree. They could not marry. (This was added without Miss McNeil's knowledge.)

George Bennett wrote an interesting letter to Warden Wolfer shortly before the bill was put into motion (only a part of it appears here):

I did not ascertain the whereabouts of the boys yesterday. I phoned Shurmeier's office but he was not in and the clerk claimed to know nothing as to the whereabouts of the boys.

As I stated to you yesterday, I know that a persistent attempt was made to prejudice the men against me, and as I believe with some degree of success. I determined however not to permit it to change my course in the lest, but to do all in my power for them, regardless of their personal feelings toward me, and trusting that time, and their better understanding of the situation after release would make everything all right.

At any rate, I did not propose to waste thought, time and nerve power in writing the letters and making visits, in order to keep myself "squared" as it were.

One of the severe criticisms passed upon my course by a certain few friends was that I insisted on refusing to pander to the wishes and to see the influence of policemen, detectives, gamblers and saloon men. My idea being that if I could not bring relief through the influence of the. . . .

It appears that Jim and Cole were already suspicious of the degree of Bennett's involvement and what he was to propose. The Judge, however, pressed on. Deedee relates:

All of this apparently was thought out as he, the judge, made the two-hour trolley ride to Stillwater. This was to be his method of action; confident he could proceed with his plan without being suspect as the mastermind behind his well plotted coup de grace.

Talking to the Boys, having them read the letters, the Judge subtly endeavored to induce Cole to take the initiative in suggesting procedure against Miss Muller, supporting Jim as usual, would agree to whatever Cole proposed.

Jim, seeing through the judge's maneuvering, shrewd as it was supposed to be, surprised the judge by his sharp, explosive response. "As I am involved with Cora Lee in this annoyance by Miss Muller, it is none of Cole's concern at the moment. Therefore, allow me to make the decision you hope for. Just go ahead with your already devised plans to protect Cora Lee, regardless of Cole or me. Whatever happens to our hopes is not in the picture. Miss Muller is not only insane, she is very dangerous."

Cole agreed with Jim fully, adding that he too felt Miss Muller was a menace to all three of them, including himself. He could not resist the opportunity to tease Jim, saying humorously, "If that female is a sample of brides of heaven, I'll remain a happy one-r."

Shortly after this the parole bill was submitted to the Legislature by Sen. Geo. P. Wilson and Rep. P.C. Deming, and sent to the board of prison managers, being approved by them and passed, as Warden Wolfer called attention to the Younger's prison record.

In all the years of their imprisonment, there was never a moment's uneasiness as to their conduct or a complaint registered by a prison official or inmate. They had accepted and complied with all rules without question and were always perfect gentlemen.

Someone had finally been successful in securing what so many had worked so long and hard for: Cole and Jim's parole. Unfortunately, it took scheming and the withholding of facts and emotions to see it through. Once again, the ever-loyal Jim Younger had put his best interests behind to protect someone he loved. He took Alix Muller's veiled threat to harm Cora Lee seriously; he sincerely believed she was mentally unbalanced and would stop at nothing to get what she wanted. Loving Cora Lee as he did, he would do whatever was in his power to keep her safe. Even if the consequences were dire.

As for the Youngers, offers of employment and help for Jim and Cole were sent to Warden Wolfer's office. One, dated July 12, 1901, was from Edward Schurmeier:

I have the following proposals to make to you in regard to the employment of the Younger brothers:

1st I will furnish them a fine store in a suitable location for a cigar and tobacco business. They can run the business in my name. I will furnish them a first class man to help them run the store. They, the Youngers, to have all the profits or on shares as they see fit. I will see to it that they have the necessary money for the business and they can make my home their home.

2nd If they are employed at the Andrew Schoch Grocery Co. they can also make my home their home. (The Andrew Schoch proposition is forwarded to you by same mail. He will give them to start with $60.00 a piece and put them at some congenial occupation. I can highly recommend Mr. Schoch as a Christian gentleman, kind and humane and one for whom it would be a pleasure to work.)

3rd If you employ them anywhere in St. Paul I will offer them my home as their home. As you are aware my residence is very retired; bounded on Central Ave., Robert St., and Aurora Ave. across from the Convent of Visitation and very little exposed to the public. I have a library of 1000 volumes which in their leisure time they could make use of.

That all sounded good, if it was proved to be a legitimate offer. When Cole heard the news of the granting of parole, he was overwhelmed. Jim was so overcome that he couldn't bring himself to go with Cole to Deputy Warden Jack Glennon's office to talk about it. He asked to wait in his cell to absorb the news and arrived in Glennon's office well after Cole.

Not knowing the time or details of their release, Jim and Cole attended Sunday chapel services the following morning. When they were told to go immediately after to Glennon's office, they did not expect to be handed civilian clothes and told that they did not have to return to their jobs. Within the hour, they would be walking out of the Prison gate.

Once outside, the dazed brothers stood stock still, looking at each other. It was hard for them to believe they were free at last. Newspaper reporters quickly descended to ask Cole and Jim their impressions as they walked the main street of Stillwater. Cole was his usual gregarious self, engaging with the men of the press. Jim kept his thoughts to himself. He would later tell the *Pioneer Press*, "I don't know what I thought. I've been keeping my feelings in check so long, ready to meet anything, that I'm afraid I didn't let myself out. But it didn't hurt me a bit."

"On July 14, 1901 (Sunday), James and Coleman T. Younger were released from Stillwater Minn. Prison," writes Deedee.

"Having served 24 years, 8 months and 3 days of a life sentence, pronounced on November 11th, 1876 (Saturday). Robert Younger passed away in Stillwater Prison Sept. 16, 1889 (Monday). For him it was a life sentence."

After walking around town for about an hour, Cole and Jim returned to the prison to have lunch with Warden Wolfer and Minneapolis representative J. W. Phillips. After lunch, accompanied by Wolfer, Glennon, and Superintendent Kilbourne of the Rochester Hospital for the Insane, the brothers took a three-hour steamboat cruise on the St. Croix River, which they enjoyed very much.

Since the parole had come so quickly, arrangements were still being made for the men's employment and lodgings. They would stay in the Warden's residence for the next few nights. Cole enjoyed visits into Stillwater the next day, but Jim was already feeling overwhelmed and chose to stay behind at the prison. Reentering society was not going to be easy for him.

"Neither Miss McNeil or Miss Muller met the Boys as they left the prison,"Deedee writes. "Cora Lee said she did not think it proper for her to do so. They would meet later, (away from the 'fanatical curious' as Jim remarked) where they were to have dinner.

"Miss Muller was ordered to stay away from the Boys, 'or else', by her editor. He had a competent reporter, a friend of the Boys and a photographer, both of whom could cover the assignment perfectly.

"As a precaution, Warden Wolfer requested Chief of Police O'Connor of St. Paul to provide a plain-clothes detective as escort to the Boys from Stillwater, merely as a precaution against any curiosity seekers.

"The detective was a friend of years standing and was also an invited dinner guest by Cora Lee. In St. Paul, the Boys registered at the same hotel with adjoining bath between the rooms. Jim said he was sure Cole's snoring had not improved with the years, not just that his loud breathing was disturbing, it was his running up and down the scales with utter disregard and perfect abandon as to the proper sequence of the musical tones or their graduated measure.

"The first electric streetcar ride was a tremendous novelty to both Cole and Jim. They had never seen one, only as pictured in magazines and newspapers. Electric lights were used in some of the prison buildings, the rest burned gas, familiar to the Boys.

"Arriving at Cora Lee's, Cole and the detective remained on the veranda, exchanging bandage with reporters. Jim entered Cora Lee's home alone, the first time since that long ago time in late Aug. of 1876.

"That meeting of Aug. 1901 was witnessed by no other living soul, that hour was theirs. The world was as though it had never existed beyond or before that greeting. The entire world was completely shut out. Nether Cora Lee or Jim ever revealed the overwhelming emotions that engulfed them, restrained for years, now to be shared together for a few fleeting moments, then to be hidden again from the world's inquisitive eyes. "

Cole and Jim had received many offers of employment but for some reason, Warden Wolfer decided that they should work for the P. N. Peterson Granite Company of Stillwater. The Peterson Company produced tombstones. For $60.00 a month, Jim would work in the office selling tombstones and Cole would travel throughout the county doing the same. The irony would not be lost on Jim; he likely detested his job.

On August 14, Jim wrote a letter to Warden Wolfer advising him that a "big, ignorant duffer" named Bloom, who also worked for Peterson, was passing himself off as Cole. Jim asked that Wolfer "call him down."

Jim was injured in a buggy accident while working for Peterson. He wrote Warden Wolfer on August 26:

I left the horse and buggy at Cambridge and come to St. Paul Saturday evening at Six o'clock and will return in the early tomorrow. Some one here is trying to keep up this Younger howl by starting the foolish report that first Cole, and then Jim, were going to get married. These men have been to see me but I was not in, and I will not be, to answer foolish questions.

On September 1, he wrote another letter to Wolfer:

I am in Bob Dunn's Town, Princeton. I met a host of friends. In fact I have met nothing else on my rounds. Met two men who voted against us, but they were friendly and congratulated me on my release. I am at present in bad shape from my mash up three weeks ago. But will stick right to business as long as I can walk or stand on my feet. I notice the St. Paul News is going to marry me off, whether or no. I do hope these fellows of the press will take a rest soon.

Was Jim responding to a news item Alix Muller had planted?

"After the disappointing parole bill was passed, Cole and St. Paul friends of his, the Schurmeiers ... urged that Cora Lee then write Little Mizzoura along the lines intended," writes Deedee. "Jim said no. His reason being she had worked years, using strength she could never regain—only to have her efforts go for naught by two men who looked for glory only for themselves. Meaning, of course, Cole and the Judge. 'Neither one of the two knew as much about writing as a hog knew about playing the flute,' said Jim.

"Jim further spoke against another book, saying in substance, 'There is no truth of the lurid stuff written about us. We were never outlaws from choice, only once. That's all it took, just one time to burn the brand upon us—'Outlaws.' We were fully aware the risk we took, Cole and I, in our endeavor to protect Bob.'

"Cole's idea was different: 'We have been declared outlaws ever since General Lee surrendered, so let's lend spice to the only two books we have ever authorized, Mizzoura and its sequel.'

"Mama still refused. Had she written the story as she first planned, its influence might have changed several lives. Of that Cora Lee never voiced speculation."

Missoura was a semi-fictional book about Cora Lee's youth and her involvement with Jim Younger, written to help cast a human light on Jim and Cole Younger.

"Jim spoke another time of Cole's brilliant war record, Confederate tho it was and because of many CSA records ordered destroyed by Washington, he could prove none of it," continues Deedee. "Jim felt their friends and buddies of years standing were aware of the facts. As to his own service record, he would only say 'I was only a horse soldier, saw action only long enough to become a defeated member of a hot skirmish—winding up in an Alton, Illinois army hospital a prisoner of war. That is over and best forgotten.' Jim's idea was Cole could or should rest upon his laurels of war, public history or not. Jim was against any idea of lawlessness, as a story would convey."

Jim eventually was admitted to "City Hospital" for a short stay. After that, it seems that Wolfer then realized that Jim needed to change jobs and Jim went to work in October selling cigars for the Andrew Schock Tobacco Company.

Col. Henry W. Younger, the Boy's father, had experimented in several varieties of tobacco on the family farm near Harrison-ville, Mo. Jim, always interested in the study of nature in general, had as a boy worked with Old Uncle Nate. Through his knowledge of tobacco, though he did not smoke, he turned for employment to that which he naturally felt he knew, tobacco.

It is interesting that Deedee would say that Jim did not smoke. In his parole reports, he responds yes to the question "Do you use tobacco?"

"While working for the Andrew Schock Tobacco Co. in St. Paul, he moved to another hotel, a smaller but quieter place," Deedee continues. "He said he would miss the companionship he and Cole had enjoyed for over fifty years yet he could not adjust to Cole's social pace. Their interests were no longer along the same lines. Their camaraderie was a thing of the past, regretfully."

Jim was required to fill out monthly reports to Warden Wolfer. The reports address his employment, his finances, how he spent his time, if he used tobacco or liquor, what he read, what outings he has taken, if he had any trouble with anyone and asked him to state in a general way his surroundings and prospects.

In his report to Warden Wolfer in October, he wrote he attended the state fair, so he must have been feeling somewhat better. But he said that he spent his time either at the store or at home. When asked if he had any trouble, he said, "Nothing but foolish questionings and I hold my own."

Jim felt that the reason he had been employed at the Schock Company was as an attraction to bring people into the store. His friend Dr. Withrow, from the prison, later said

> . . . he felt he was employed rather as an exhibit than as a salesman. He brooded over it. Only by sheer nerve he held on to it. I believe his worries over the fact that he was employed because of his notoriety as a former outlaw preyed on his mind . . . I do not believe [Cole] ever realized the strain under which Jim lived.

Deedee continues:

> When Cora Lee suggested he should not become an introvert, but should mingle with others, take more interest in the world about him, he replied "My Cora Lee. For a quarter of a century my life was centered in the flotsam and jetsam of a shut in world. I did what I could for my fellow beings. Perhaps I miss the serenity of my once every day existence." Continuing, "Now I find a vastly changed world, a generation gap to hurdle. Abruptly

I am expected to adjust to a world that does not know where it is going but is recklessly, rebelliously, groping, seeking to limit the size of the universe to its own inadequate intelligence, resulting in a fast falling toward a moral decadence."

Cole thought differently, telling a reporter:

After our release from prison, Jim's precarious health and his inability to rejoin his family in Missouri combined to make [his] fits of depression more frequent. While he was working . . ., instead of putting in his afternoons, which were free, among men, or enjoying the sunshine and air, which had so long been out of our reach, he would go to his room and revel in socialistic literature, which only tended to overload a mind already surcharged with troubles. For my part, I tried to get into the world again, to live down the past, and I could and did enjoy the theaters, although Jim declared he would never set foot in one until he could go a free man.

Was part of Jim's depression because he was being stalked?

"Miss Muller tried to reach Jim at the hotel before he moved,"continues Deedee. "Each time she was told he was not in. By following Cole one evening, she located Jim's new lodgings and continued her phone calls, only to be told he was not in.

"Then she left letters at the desk, in person, not daring to mail them. One afternoon, the manager was at the desk when Miss Muller asked for Jim. When the manager said he was not in, she demanded his key, saying, 'We are about to be married and as I will be living here, I wish to see the room. I'll wait there for him.'

"The manager replied, 'Madam, this may come as a big disappointment to you, but I don't believe a word of what you just said. My hotel is for men only and no exceptions. I am quite familiar with the Younger case. Now shall I call the police or will you leave under your own steam?' Miss Muller departed in haste.

"Shortly after this episode, Jim's 'shine boy' asked, 'Mr. Jim, do you know some woman is tagging you? She hangs around across the street from your hotel. When you come out, she starts right after you.' Jim suggested she could be watching someone else, but the boy was insistent. 'No siree. I sure nuff know what I see most every day or evening.'

"Jim had suspected Miss Muller was doing just that. Returning to his hotel one evening, he strolled along Ramsey Street, leisurely window-shopping. Looking back along the street, he glimpsed Miss Muller darting into a doorway. Impulsively, his intent was to face her brazenness once and for all time. Instinctively, he sensed that was her motive. In doing so, he would be going to her! She could and would undoubtedly turn his action to her own advantage.

"Slowly resuming his walk without showing further interest in her trailing ability, formulating three letters he would write and mail as soon as he reached his room.

"The first was to Warden Wolfer. Explaining the episode of Miss Muller earlier in the evening, he asked the warden permission to move to Minneapolis. Should Maj. Elwin reply favorably to his request for a position, which he felt sure the Major would assure him was open, and he would check in the Hoffman House, a family hotel, Mrs. Hoffman the owner being a friend of the Boys as well as Cora Lee.

"The Warden and the Major answered promptly, favorably, and under the circumstances both felt it a wise move, knowing of Miss Muller's past endeavors.

"With the hotel manager's help, Jim left by the back door, his baggage to follow by express. In relating the story later told to Cora Lee, he said he and the manager enjoyed playing the role of two small boys escaping after an orchard invasion.

"Eventually it dawned on Miss Muller Jim had eluded her. Frantic calls to Cole's hotel resulted in being told to contact Chief O'Connor. Cole ignored her letters.

"One Sunday shortly after the boys arrived at Cora Lee's house, she answered the doorbell, opening the door to Miss Muller. Without waiting to be invited, she pushed the door wide open with a bang, barged into the living room as both men arose.

"Seeing Jim across the room, Miss Muller rushed to him before he was aware of her intentions. She threw her arms around his neck, shouting hysterically, shouting 'Jim, my love, my darling.' Jim struggled to push her away, but it was Cole, who not too gently forced her to a chair across the room, saying, 'You are crazier than I thought you were. Don't you know you can be arrested for disturbing the peace?'

"Sobbing wildly, shaking a fist at Cora Lee, Miss Muller shouted, 'I hate you. You are a devil. Because of you, he will not confess his love for me. I will kill myself if he continues to ignore me and refuses to see me. You will be blamed.'

"She further announced, 'I have his letters saying you took him away from me. My paper will publish them.'

"Cora Lee said gently, 'Miss Muller. That is such a wildly exaggerated statement for you to make. I can only say to take your life is, of course, an idle threat that is so meaningless. Taking your life, you would never know what, if anything, you had gained by such an utterly futile deed, to say the least. It shows your lack of clear thinking. You are to be pitied for making such an inane and stupid remark. I do feel sorry for you.'

"Turning to Cole, Miss Muller said, 'You don't believe I have letters, do you.' 'No, I do not,' Cole emphatically replied. 'Jim has repeatedly stated he never wrote you a line in his life. He even refused you his autograph, which you asked for, the first time he ever saw you.'

"'You may have letters from me when I was asinine enough to inquire about your friends in high places you bragged about, that could help us, but you never produced them. If you expect to use them, you won't get very far.'

"Miss Muller was still not convinced. 'I don't care what you say. I warn you all, I will kill myself.' She repeated the words several times.

"Jim was silent all through the argument. Crossing the room, he stood looking at her intently. She seemed to shrink in her chair. All the arrogance had left her for the moment. She did not look *at* him as he spoke. His voice, as always, courteous yet his meaning clear.

"'Miss Muller,' he said. 'I am amazed at your maudlin ravings. You have created a monstrous falsity, a fabrication of your own sick mind. This is the third time I have spoken to you in all the years you have annoyed me with your unwelcome, unsolicited intrusion into my life.' Continuing he said, 'You have no indisputable evidence to substantiate your ridiculous claims of letters from me. I too could say I am sorry for you. That would not be true coming from me. I am not. I have no feeling for you. I am not in love with you. I never have been. I wouldn't marry you if you were the last woman on earth, were I free to do so, which you know I am not.'

"After a moment he continued. 'Now I will do some warning. Unless you stop all this harassment of Miss McNeil, Cole and myself, I can promise you, that with all you have done to all three of us in the past, I will take steps to have you placed where you will no longer annoy anyone. You better leave now before I really tell you what I think of you. Bud," he grinned at Cole. 'Will you do the honors, see Miss Muller to the inter-urban?'

"Cole was amazed at Jim's using his boyhood name of 'Bud'. Returning Jim's grin with a broader one, as he almost lifted Miss Miller from her chair, he said, 'It will pleasure me Brother Damie.' Heading the defeated Miss Muller from the hall, he hurried her through the door held open by Cora Lee.

"Walking to the streetcar, Cole asked how she made the trip from St. Paul without his seeing her. 'I was watching your hotel at seven o'clock. I followed you to your breakfast, then to the inter-urban, got on the second car. In Minneapolis, I saw Jim meet you when you both got on the Chicago Ave. car. I knew where you were going. I waited for the next car. I have done it before without you seeing me.' This was said with an air of assurance as she made the statement in a loud, harsh voice.

"Downtown, Cole saw her on the Express, waited until it left, knowing she could not get off until it reached St. Paul.

"Cole visited the Schurmeiers and as Miss Muller kept in touch with them also, Mrs. Schurmeier kept Cole informed of her conversational topics and of course it was Jim. Her ego never lessened. On one of Cole's visits, Mrs. Schurmeier told Cole Miss Muller still stubbornly clung to the belief Jim would turn to her and declare his love for her.

"The very fact that I know he is lonely and longs for me is one reason I am sure of him. In my own way I will make him admit his love for me and soon,' she declared.

"Cole laughed as he listened to Mrs. Schurmeier. 'You can tell that blue-stocking for me that my brother is not about to admit to something that is not true. Not Jim Younger, he isn't built that way. She is wasting her time, but it's her time, I reckon.'

"The summer [had] passed peacefully, Jim at Cora Lee's often on Sunday afternoons. Miss Muller attempted no more open demonstrations so far as Jim knew. Only once did the boys see her. Jim had gone to St. Paul to see Cole. As they came out of Cole's hotel, she stood at the street corner. Turning quickly, she hurried to board a streetcar. Cole asked Jim, 'Does seeing her bother you?' Jim answered, 'Only about like meeting Jesse James.' Cole dropped the subject. To all appearances, Jim did not dwell on the past hysteria of Miss Muller. It was, he said, a bad dream from which he had at long last awakened and forgotten.

"Late in Sept. 1901, Cora Lee revealed her plans to marry Judge Bennett and make their home in the Black Hills!

"Cora Lee McNeil Deming and George Morris Bennett were to be married on her birthdate, Oct. 18th 1901 in Lead, So. Dakota. She was to leave Minneapolis, Minn. Oct. 7th, 1901 (Monday) for Kansas City, Mo. Then on to the Black Hills.

"On Sunday, Oct. 6th 1901, Jim Younger called on Cora Lee, expressing his regret at not being able to see her at the depot the next morning. Cora Lee's train departing at 8:30 a.m., he having an appointment in St. Paul at 8:00 a.m. in regard to his old position made it impossible to see her off. Cora Lee understood and shared her disappointment.

" 'I am returning to my old hotel tonight,' Jim explained. 'There is no reason for my remaining here in Minneapolis after today.' Noting her questioning look, he assured her by saying, 'She won't bother me while I am alive and know what's going on.' He referred to Miss Muller. 'Chief O'Connor told me over the telephone yesterday,' Jim continued. 'That one of his men had served a Superior Court order restraining her activities where I am concerned, with an added "or else" from the Chief.'

"He would see Cole more often, as well as a small coterie of friends he enjoyed being with.

"His stay was brief. Both made the supreme effort to suppress the heartache of parting, yet it was there, deep within them, tensely guarded against sudden acknowledgment, each fully aware it was their last hour together.

"Holding her hands firmly in his, close to her heart, Jim stood for several moments looking down at his Cora Lee intently, as though to impose her image upon his innermost self. Then kissing each palm, folding her fingers over them, he said reverently, 'God bless these tiny hands that have done so much for me.'

"'For all that you and I have shared together in this life for such a little while, I shall always be thankful. God has been so good to me. I have been truly blessed all the long, lonely years, in the knowledge of your steadfast love, unspoken, unwritten. Your understanding, sympathy, and faithfulness have been the only means by which I have retained my trust in God and my sanity.'

"Again he stood with eyes closed as though in prayer. When he spoke, his voice almost broke with intensity. 'Some day, my corona. There will be no chasms, no insurmountable bluffs, no raging torrent between us. To say time heals all things is erroneous with me. It never can. All that remains of a future for me lies far in that world of the four noble truths, Nirvana, on the Plains of Deva Chan.'

"Gently he released her hands and without another word, turned, opened the door. With head bowed, he crossed the wide veranda, descended the steps to the sidewalk. Slowly, with his head still bowed, he walked to the corner, not once looking back to see Cora Lee standing alone watching with tear blurred eyes as he boarded the streetcar that carried him out of her life, not to be reunited until after 'Mayra.'

"Cora Lee hid her heartache from a prying, curious world. Never word was said against the man she married, even though in time, she learned of his intrigue, unknown to her until after the Younger bill was passed, directly designed toward Jim and his hopes for a full pardon, or at least the right to live a normal life, even on parole.

"In all the years of Cora Lee's marriage to Judge Bennett, she shared whatever hardship, sorrow or joy he faced. She voiced no complaint when he mismanaged her small fortune unwisely nor would she permit her children to criticize, what to them was his utter lack of responsibility for her loss as well as theirs.

"When Judge Bennett passed away Dec. 25th 1925, Cora Lee was the remaining member of the eternal triangle, but it was not until 1939 that she partially drew aside the curtain that concealed the tremendous love between Cora Lee and Jim Younger, spanning then over sixty years of their lives. In so doing, there was not the slightest intimidation of reproach to her husband's unethical conduct.

"The evidence was there, clearly, needing no cogency of proof actually stated by Cora Lee in words. She had known, mainly by intuition, often by remarks, shortly after her marriage, that her husband to be had devised the plot against Jim before the parole bill was passed.

"Realizing he would never have the love that Cora Lee held for Jim Younger, despite the excessive pressure he put upon her by his constant reminders of the enormous and tireless efforts he had taken upon himself by his intruding own idea for her and the Boys without remuneration, the Judge was filled with a jealous desire for revenge, to exact his pound of flesh. She had retained her serenity.

"By cunningly suggesting to Justice Stark that a conditional amendment could be added to the parole bill, handed down by the Chief Justice, verbally, banning marriage by any person on parole, Judge Bennett cleverly avoided involvement, publically, other than being the author of the original parole bill as written, then passed by the board. No credit was given to Cora Lee for her part in drafting the petition.

"Chief Justice Start promptly seized upon the covert innuendo to vent his own displeasure at being the only dissenter on the parole board, and had the satisfaction of the support of the board.

"Had Jim looked back that sunny afternoon of Oct. 1901 to see the small lonely figure standing so alone, watching as he boarded the street car, life would have been hopefully, entirely changed not only for Cora Lee and Jim Younger, but several other lives vitally concerned would have been happily different.

"Undoubtedly, Cora Lee would have tossed all her plans to the four winds; would have fought on bravely for the pardon that came too late for Jim and his Corona.

"Jim Younger did not look back. Why? Only in that far off Silence in Nirvana, on the Plains of Deva Chan, will the answer be found when the scrolls are unrolled and the 'Four Noble Truths' are also revealed."

In another letter, Deedee writes:

Cora Lee was disillusioned soon after her marriage to the Judge. Her heartache over the whole thing, she hid from the world but not from her daughter. Altho Cora Lee never uttered a word of reproach toward her husband, daughter was not exactly dumb or stupid as to the facts. For twenty years the Youngers were not mentioned in our home, until years after the Judge passed on.

CHAPTER 12
End of the Road

JIM MADE NO MENTION ON THE LOSS OF CORA LEE BUT IN A LETTER
to his parole office F. A. Whittier shortly after she left, Jim com-
plained about other ex-cons bothering him for money. He wrote:

One fellow said he was paralyzed, and I replied—blow your
whiskey breath the other way or I will be paralyzed also. He
went out very mad but he was cured. Fear not for me, for
these fellows have got the wrong man.

Whittier replied:

Both of your letters of recent date duly received, and I am
please to know that you are getting on well.

Do not allow the ex-convicts to bother you. If they ask
you to do anything that you think you ought not to do,
plainly tell them. I do not think, however, I need to give
you this advise as you are very thoroughly grounded in this
particular and I know you do not fear to speak up plainly
and to the point whenever moral courage is in demand.
I am satisfied that you will get along well and that you are
sure to prosper.

If Jim had just lost the love of his life, it is interesting to note two comments on his November 20, 1901, report to Warden Wolfer. Jim writes that he has been enjoying "Sunday dinners with my best girl." Was he thinking of previous weeks, before Cora Lee left? Or was there someone else? His statement in that portion of the report fits well with his statement marked "Remarks": "Am gaining health and flesh. And full of good cheer." How could he be of good cheer when Cora Lee had recently moved to the Black Hills to be married?

This is where the great mystery of Jim's involvement with Alix Muller becomes even more complicated. If all of these events with Alix actually happened, as Cora Lee communicated them to her daughter, would Jim be interested in actually having a relationship with Alix after Cora Lee was out of the picture? Yes, there is that possibility.

Alix wrote a letter to Governor Van Sant, dated January 8, 1902. She began her letter, "Please do not regard this as a formal appeal to the Pardon board, but simply as a heart to heart statement—a woman's prayer for mercy to whom she loves." She asks that Jim Younger be allowed to marry her, so the two can live out their lives in happiness.

Few people in Jim's life had good things to say about Alix Muller. However, it might be possible that after Cora Lee left to be married, the ever-persistent Miss Muller took that opportunity to connect with Jim, who no doubt was very lonely and depressed. It might be that Jim spent time with her after Cora Lee left but eventually realized that Cora Lee was his true love and there was no place in his life for Alix.

Confusing matters is a letter Jim wrote to Warden Wolfer. Although Jim was meticulous in his letter writing, always following proper form, this letter is not dated. We don't know to whom Jim

might be inferring when he wrote, seemingly in reference to Cora
Lee and her children:

With my report, I send you this note in confidence.

I have hoped for just a few years of married life, with
wife, children to love, and to make me happy—all to make
them happy in return.

But I cannot marry while on parole, and long for freedom, to enable me to take this step as soon as possible.

Warden Wolfer was aware of both Cora Lee McNeil and
Alix Muller. Yet he was a friend of Cora Lee, so it would not have
seemed unnatural if Jim stated her name in this letter, if that was
to whom he referred. On the other hand, Jim was very private and
at this point was also being protective of Cora Lee, so leaving her
name out of it is understandable as well.

On September 10, 1902, before the departure and marriage of
Cora Lee, Jim wrote to the editor of the *Minneapolis Times*:

Out of courtesy to one unable to express himself, kindly
refrain from all mention of a pardon sought by the
Younger brothers until you have first consulted me on the
subject.

While Jim still hoped for a pardon, which would then leave
him free to marry Cora Lee, he did not want to be a part of the
campaign to secure it. He was still looking out for Cora Lee's best
interests and not his own.

If Alix Muller did intend to eventually marry Jim, it would
seem that she would continue to stand by his side. Especially since
Jim was obviously having a hard time living the life he had been

left to endure until such time he might be granted a pardon. But Alix didn't do that. Alix left St. Paul to take up residence in Idaho, saying she didn't like the attention from the press that surrounded Jim; the attention of the press that she herself had sometimes created and basked in. It seems very possible that Jim finally told Alix she could never replace Cora Lee in his affection and this was what caused her to leave St. Paul.

Another possibility arises in regard to Jim's attention toward each woman, however, Jim had been suffering from depression for a very long time. Cole later stated:

The bullet wound which Jim received in our last fight near Madelia, shattering his upper jaw, remaining imbedded near his brain . . . affected Jim at intervals all his prison life, and he would have periodical spells of depression, during which he would give up all hope, and his gloomy spirits would repel the sympathy of those who were disposed to cheer him up.

Jim's depression no doubt increased when he "lost" his Cora Lee. Is it possible that what Jim wrote in his reports was a figment of his imagination, born of his depression and his weakening mind?

In his report of January 1902, Jim writes of being ill several days. In his next report, he contradicts his earlier reports of going to the fair and a play and writes that he has not attended any event since his parole. He says he is "at work when not sick." By this time, he no longer worked for Andrew Schock's company but instead was working for Colonel James Elwin in his store, selling cigars.

In his very brief report of March 20, he says he went to hear "Sousa's band" the day before. He also says he is reading periodicals only. It seems he had put aside the books he had always loved to read. He went to the "Grand Opera in the Palace of the King" in

April. He said he was "very well" satisfied with his job. In June, he went to the "Metropolitan," but only once.

Later in June, Elwin sold his store and Jim was out of a job. He wrote to Wolfer that he "needed work."

Jim wrote to Warden Wolfer again: "I am asked daily what Cole is doing and I do not know. Which leaves me in an awkward or foolish position. Please let me know."

On August 24, Jim wrote the following letter to Warden Wolfer:

The greatest difficulty I have had to meet is the erroneous idea that I have money to burn, where as I have had the hardest kind of a time to keep up to an even notch. Elkins, Bronaugh, Prather, Jones, my nephew, have all, according to newspapers, sent me checks but the truth of the matter is that they talked but forgot the check. Jones is the only one who ever sent me a check and for 100$ when I was sick one year ago and I have heard so much of that check and of Charles Jones likability that I have many times, from the depth of my soul, wished that I had never heard of it.

I wrote Elkins, Bronaugh, Prather and a few other talking friends but to this day, not one of them have replied. And if Cole has received any checks, he knows but I do not for he has not acquainted me with the fact. And again, my board bill is higher than the average because I have so much trouble in getting food that I can eat. At the Fremont House, where Col. Elwin placed me, was a good meat and bread hotel but I would have starved to death there. Lots of these friends that talk, for publication, have finished their part when their boastings have been printed. Just like Ed Schwermeier's published offer of a home and business.

Jim was offered a good position as an insurance writer for Sam Johnston of St. Paul. As Johnston waited for his license to be cleared, Jim remained idle (although he said on his report that he had worked fifteen days at a dollar a day.)

A letter dated September 29, 1902, to Warden Wolfer from Jim's parole office F. A. Whittier reads:

After I saw you the last time you were here, I got a note from Jim Younger in which he said that he was waiting for the Insurance Co. to obtain their license and that he would be at work in a day or two. I heard nothing from him until a day or two ago when he wrote a very doleful letter saying that he had nothing to do and no way to make a living. I have succeeded in finding him employment with F. R. Yerxa & Co. of this city. Have been to see Mr. Yerxa this morning and he will put him to work at something, either in the cigar counter or as a salesman on the floor. Have sent for Jim to come over at once.

Wolfer responded to Whittier the following day:

Yours of the 29th, advising the disposition made of Jas. Younger is received. I am glad to hear that you have at last found employment for him and I hope he can make a go of it. He seems to be nearly as helpless as a baby. I cannot understand how he has been able to support himself during the long period he has been out of employment unless he receives help from some source other than he has been able to provide for himself.

I think it might be well to keep in pretty close touch with him from now on and if he cannot hold his present position or something else that will enable him to support himself, I believe it would be a very good idea for him to return here until such time as something definite may be developed for him.

Several people were trying to help Jim, but he grew more and more despondent. It seems that he was not an active participant in Cole's life at this point. Cole was enjoying working for Police Chief John O'Connor, where a lot of his time was spent chatting to all who would engage him. Jim wrote:

Please let me hear from you, for I do not wish to be idle or to loose the time. Cole, I hear, is sick, but I do not know where he lives and would not like going around imagining so keep still.

It all came crashing down when Jim was told that his job writing insurance couldn't become a reality. As an ex-con, his signature on a legal document meant nothing. In the eyes of the state, those on parole were considered "dead" in the legal world. For Jim, who had already been feeling dead, the state all but confirmed his emotion.

Cole denied that he and Jim weren't seeing each other or that Jim had any reason to imply that he didn't know where he was living. He said he wasn't pleased with Jim's appeal for a full pardon the year before, or of his "love affair," but as far as he was concerned all was well between them.

"I know Jim was very despondent because the pardon board did not grant our full pardon at their last session," Cole told the *Kansas City Star*. "But he did not view this matter in the right light. He thought that we should have been allowed to go home at once. It is the rule of the pardon board, however, not to terminate a parole for a year. This is right and proper and I frequently told Jim he should try and be contented until the expiration of this time."

Jim continued to criticize Warden Wolfer and now-Governor Van Sant and said that he felt that he had been treated unfairly and that they didn't seem to have his best interests at heart.

"The criticisms he made about Governor Van Sant and Warden Wolfer in his last letter was awfully unwarranted," Cole lamented. "Warden Wolfer was our best friend, while we were in prison and out. If it had not been for Warden Wolfer we would still be in prison."

Cole felt Jim had "been acting queerly for several months." He said that he felt some of his actions could only be accounted for on the grounds that his mind had "become weakened." "He never regained his cheerful mood, for when he was up, he was away up, and when down, away down. There was no half way place with Jim."

Could Jim have been bi polar? The contents of his monthly parole reports are certainly inconsistent, with one month being favorable and the next illustrating that he is in a deep depression.

Warden Wolfer claimed that he felt Jim had been bordering on insanity for some time. He had noted the changes in Jim's "manner"; how he had become aggressive and felt that the bullet that had been lodged near his brain for all those years had caused his brain to "give away."

Chief of Police John O'Connor later claimed that Jim had been slowly going insane over the past year. E. J. Schurmeier said he was positive that "Jim's mind had long been impaired."

John Whitaker met with Jim after he was told about the job falling through. He later told the *Kansas City Star*

"Younger began by informing me that he had been offered a job by an insurance company to write insurance. He said the job suited him first-rate and that he had signed a contract. But when the company came to look up the matter, it found that Jim could not write insurance because he was supposed to be dead and his name on an application for insurance cut no more figure than a fly speck.

'And that's the way of it', Jim said. 'I'm a mere nothing in the world's affairs from now on, old man. I'm a ghost—the ghost of Jim Younger. Who was a man—not an extra good one—but I'm nothing. Walking 'round here people might suppose I was alive, and if it was on the square, I could write insurance with the best of them. But I'm as dead as Caesar. The insurance company has informed me that it has satisfied itself of my legal non-existence.*"

Whitaker asked Jim why he didn't resume working at a tobacco company or take another job where he didn't have to interact with people so much. Jim responded:

Well, I am a man of action. I always was from my youth. What I need is something to do that will give me a game to beat. This thing of standing behind a rail and playing polite to a lot of men who are worse of heart than I ever was is not to my liking. It might be something worthwhile if Jim Younger, ex-raider and convict, should turn out to be the best insurance man in the state. You see, I'm hardly the same man I was when I went into the state prison. In the library, I read nearly everything that was ever printed about the soul and its manifestations. The fact is, I believe there is nothing left of me but the soul I started with. I should like to win at something, but all the rest, Quantrill and the old game of fight and war, are just as remote as if they had been another man's experiences. If they would let me be Jim Younger, I'd start under the handicap and beat it before I quit. No man is all bad, you know. Every last rascal on earth has a good spot in him somewhere. Scientific education will do away with penitentiaries some of these days, but I'm dead.

Was this the ravings of an insane man, or of a man who had simply had enough and was severely depressed? And certainly the two emotions can go hand in hand. Once again, Jim put his thoughts on paper in a letter to Cora Lee.

Deedee mentioned to Wilbur Zink the first letter she read, the one she believed she was meant to see was a significant one in the Jim-Cora Lee story:

The import of the entire letter was significantly expressive, revealing a Jim Younger that only his "Corona, his M.S.R." would understand and love.

The letter dated October 18 1902, opened with "Corona, My Soul Reward. A long, lonely year has passed for me since you took the momentous step we both felt to be best for you and your three children. You could not have gone on alone, as frail as you are.

The promise made to you as to the fatherly care, responsibility and education of your children was far beyond anything I could offer at the time under the adverse, existing circumstances. My desire to do was nonetheless sincere, prayerfully hoped for, ending in a

Dreamers dream. As to what the years ahead will bring, one can only wonder.

I have longed to win at some one thing, have earnestly tried. If when I left Stillwater the world had let me be just Jim Younger, I could have made a new beginning under any and all handicaps. I would have beaten them all before I quit.

A life sentence behind bars can tie knots in any man's soul, make scars that constantly burn unless he is strong enough to make the adjustment, quickly, necessary from the life he once knew before the storm struck, so that he finds behind bars, leaving the world outside the high walls while he pays his debt to society, relentlessly demanding its pound of flesh.

No one can help him in that transition. He must make it alone, but with the knowledge there is someone who loves and understands him, eases the struggle. You, my Cora Lee, gave me both but without a full pardon, I fervently prayed for. . . ."

For twelve years I was librarian in Stillwater prison. During those years I sent for and read all the literature I could find on the Soul and its manifestations. At this moment, all that knowledge is of no use to me.

I have endeavored to forge a link between the world of the few years of happiness and hopes I once knew and the one around me, with its struggling masses, all of them like me, striving for a mere existence. But as for me, it only resulted in the battle for a Lost Cause in the maelstrom of my life.

As I walk about, no doubt people suppose I am alive but legally I am as dead as the mighty Caesar, non-existent, a mere nothing in the fast moving affairs of the world. A ghost, the ghost of Jim Younger, who was once a man, though perhaps not a very good one.

Now comes the realization, alarmingly, I am no longer self-reliant, not as I once was. Like an old sponge, I have been so thoroughly compressed I am completely devoid of the will to do.

Instead of expanding and achieving, in growing older, I shrink. Any metal alertness I may have once possessed I seem to have misplaced, along with my former power of self-guidance.

Nothing remains of "Me" but the Soul I started life with. Over half a century away from the present, that Soul is housed in a body that is but a dry shell, not equal to the task now demanded of it.

Long ago I made my first move in a sequence of events. The end, I was positive I could see clearly. It could have been an old pattern, but it was strange and new to me. At the time, I endeavored to change the course of converging events. Mine was as a voice crying alone in the wilderness. No one heeded my wailings.

In ages past, someone much wiser than I questioned "wherefore is the remedy, O ye silent Host, ye who in habit illimitable space? Have ye no answer? For me, my Cora Lee, only the echo, 'No answer' comes back.

I do not presume to judge as to your marriage being right or wrong. I do ask that you believe me, always remembering this, my promise to you, My Soul's Reward" that—

"Somewhere on this moving planet, in the midst of years to be.

In the Sunlight and in the shadows, waits a loving heart for Thee.

Sometime in that far off silence, you will feel my van-
ished hand.
Then in that far off somewhere, only then, shall we
know all.
All that now we cannot understand."

Deedee writes:

Following those lines comes a sketch at the bottom of the
page, on the right, instead of its usual place at the top right.
The profile of the "Old Fool" was drawn as though looking
through a fine mist or thin clouds. Left across the page was
entirely blank, no cliff, no chasm, no raging torrents, no
waving grass, no profile of Corona, M.S.R. It was signed
"Con Amour, The Old Fool. Jim Younger Oct 18th 1902."
    I do not know if these lines [of poetry] were original
with Jim Younger or by some unknown author. I never saw
them before or since so can give no credit.

That was the last letter Jim Younger ever wrote. On Sunday,
October 19, 1902, Jim Younger's body was found in his St. Paul
hotel room with a bullet through his head from the gun at his side.
The Coroners verdict was "*Death by suicide, sometime before midnight
of October 18, 1902.*" That date was the birthday and first wedding
anniversary of Cora Lee McNeil Deming Bennett.
    Two notes were found in Jim's room. On his dresser lay an
envelope stuffed with letters from Alix. On the back of the envelope was written:

To all that is good and true, I love and bid farewell. Jim
Younger

On the other side as written,

"Oh, Lassie, good-by. All relatives just stay away from me. No crocodile tears wanted. Reporters: Be my friend. Burn me up" Jim Younger.

Were the comments referring to Alix? It would seem that since so many knew of Alix's love for Jim that naming her would finally reveal and demonstrate his love for her. Or were his words referring to Cora Lee, the woman he loved and protected from public scandal? Was he leaving the letters from Alix as a sign to Cora Lee that Alix continued to try to be an integral and negative role in his life? Jim didn't say.

As to asking his relatives to stay away and not offer "crocodile tears," it is evident that Jim considered himself completely alone. Was this a message for Cole, the brother he sometimes felt abandoned by as Cole took to his new life without the problems Jim endured? Did "burn me up" mean that Jim wished to be cremated, totally leaving the body that caused him so much pain? Cole thought otherwise. He later wrote, "I think the 'burn me up' was an admonition to the reporters. Jim always felt the papers had been bitter to us, although some of them had been staunch supporters of the proposal to our parole."

In Jim's final hour, he chose to write a statement that he placed next to the envelope.

October 18—Last night on earth. So good-by Lassie, for I will think of thee. A.U.G. Forgive me, for this is my only chance. I have done nothing wrong. But politics are all that Van Sant, Wolfer and others care for. Let the people judge. Treat me right and fair, reporters for I am a square man.

A Socialist and decidedly for women's rights. Bryan is the brightest man these United States has ever produced. His one mistake was in not coming out for all the people and absolute socialism. Come out, Bryan. There is no such thing as a personal God. God is universal, and I know him well, and am not afraid. I have pity for the pardoning board: they do not stop to consider their wives or to think of the man who knows how to love and appreciate a friend in truth. Good-by sweet lassie.

Sharing some of his political beliefs in his final words seems to demonstrate that Jim Younger continued to believe that he had always been an honest and forthright man. Even though he thought he did not have the respect of others to have them care what he thought or said.

Although Jim was a beaten man, apparently reveling in his loneliness and unacceptable (to him) fate, he was a proud man as well. Had he not been suffering depression to such a great magnitude, he probably would not have liked the attention his suicide was bound to bring. He wouldn't have liked to go out as someone so woeful that he took the easy way out. Jim did not tolerate pity. Yet here it was. An act that demonstrated that Jim was so depressed that everything that had driven his life didn't matter anymore. All that was over.

Cole was in bed sick when he was told of Jim's final act. It appears that he was not too surprised. He gave a statement to the press, saying, "It is too bad. We have had so much trouble that it seems unusually hard to bear at this time. I believe Jim was temporarily insane."

On October 23, Cole wrote to Lizzie Daniel about Jim's death. He said he had seen Jim a few days before his death and "knew he was insane." Cole said that if he had reported that fact, Jim would have been sent back to prison, something that Warden Wolfer had said might be better for Jim. Cole told Lizzie that all through his life, Jim had come to Cole with his problems. "But during the last year he went to no one but Miss Muller and I let them go their way. I did my best to get him to go out with me until I found out Miss Muller did not want him to go."

It would seem that apparently Jim was in *some* sort of relationship with Alix Muller at that time.

Jim's body was taken to O'Halloran & Murphy, undertakers. A large crowd gathered, hoping to see the dead outlaw's body but they were denied that opportunity.

A strange letter was sent to Henry Wolfer from someone representing the Great Northern Railway Line:

Wouldn't it help the Parole Board, including the Warden, in their strenuous efforts to gain a little more of the cheap notoriety they are so desirous of obtaining, to embalm Mr. James Younger's body & place it in front of the public with the monogram of that would-be Honorable— distinguished—notoriety loving body inscribed on a tablet of leather underneath—We hold everything but his breath & we wish we had that.

Deedee writes that Alix Muller returned to St. Paul (although how she would have been able to get there so fast is questionable).

"It is true Chief of Police O'Connor of St. Paul, a personal friend of Jim and Cole, placed a special detail at the mortuary where Jim was taken," writes Deedee. "I have the version of Mr. O'Halloran, the mortician, who was a client of Judge Bennett and who wrote to Mama after Jim's body left St. Paul.

"The St. Paul Dispatch gave O'Halloran's address, as the mortuary; Chief O'Connor directed somebody for Cole who was ill. Miss Muller lost no time in getting there, demanding that she, 'as Jim's widow' be permitted to select the casket, the burial place, in fact make all the funeral arrangements.

"Mr. O'Halloran challenged her status as a widow and her reply was, 'We were married in Heaven'. Mr. O'Halloran phoned Chief O'Connor because of the disturbance she created before he and an assistant forcibly put her out of the office. The Chief sent police, who threatened her with arrest unless she left the premises."

The decisions were to be his family's. His sister, Retta Younger Rawlins, sent word from Texas that Jim's body was to be sent to Lee's Summit, Missouri, where he would be laid to rest with his mother and brother Bob. Cole agreed. One way or another, he wanted Jim to return home.

Alix Muller wrote a letter to Cole's friend Lizzie Brown Daniels that she "did not see how his relatives dared to overrule" Jim's request to be cremated and protested against his being consigned to "a lonely, unwished for, grave."

In a letter dated December 5, 1902, Alix wrote to Lizzie:

The recent terrible event which took away one who was dearer than life itself to me, must have been a very painful shock to you, knowing Jim as you did. The real cause of his death was, however, a greater tragedy than his supposed "insanity" could have been. After living a life of sacrifice, he died for the sake of others who were not even magnanimous enough to acknowledge his martyrdom. I know all, though, because I have his last letters and I will soon tell all, so that justice so long due shall at this late date be meted out to him by a thoughtless world.

Alix sent word to the St. Paul newspapers, although she had earlier claimed she had left Jim's side because of her aversion to their reporting of Jim:

He was driven to his act by his persecution. I am his wife, understand, spiritually. No scandal has ever attached itself to my name, but before God he is mine and mine alone. My life will be to place him right before the world.

Although Alix Muller had said she might attend Jim's funeral, she did not. She later asked Lizzie Daniel to put a wreath of flowers on his grave, which Lizzie did. In February 1904, Alix moved to Oklahoma City where she kept house for her stepbrother, Arthur Muller. She was writing a book titled *Lives of Great Men and Women* when she died there a short time after, in April 1904. She never publically mentioned Jim again nor did she make any effort to "place him right before the world."

His nephew-in-law C. B. Hull claimed Jim's body and his casket was taken to the train station. The following morning Jim, in body if not in soul, returned to Kansas City aboard a Chicago, St. Paul, Minneapolis, and Omaha baggage car. His casket was taken down to Lee's Summit to the home of his sister Belle's niece, Mrs. Nott Fenton, and placed on display in the parlor.

Jim Younger's funeral was held on Wednesday, October 22, at the Fenton home. His family privately said their goodbyes before opening the door to the crowd of people waiting outside. Reverend J. E. Hampton from the Baptist Church and Reverend S. F. Shiffler of the Presbyterian Church were the officiates. "Rest, Weary, Rest," a most-appropriate hymn, was sung and Reverend Hampton recited the nineteenth and twenty-seventh Psalms. Of note were remarks by Shiffler that included:

And we pray thee to remember the brother, who now sits in his lonely meditation upon the loss of a brother and a companion in the flesh, may he now turn unto thee and find thee as a brother and a friend who sticketh closer than even a brother. And we evoke thy tender mercies upon her who gave this one comfort by imparting unto him the affections of a human tender heart, and as she now grieves his loss, may she turn in her sorrow unto thee and pour out her soul and all that is within her to the praise and glory of thy holy name and she love thee even greater than him who now has fallen.

Again, did the reverend refer to Alix or Cora Lee? Neither's name was mentioned. Nor was anything personal about Jim, his struggle or the life he lived before or after his long time in the Stillwater Penitentiary. It was as if the loving, self-sacrificing, and loyal aspects of Jim had been forgotten.

After those gathered sang, "We Shall Know Each Other There," about 150 people filed past Jim's open casket. One of the reporters, seemingly one who knew Jim in his youth, described Jim's appearance:

Instead of looking upon an unshaven face, with broad and high cheek bones, they saw the features of a meek, mild appearing man, with a growth of beard four inches long tinged with gray. The forehead was high and the head partially bald. The skin back of the right ear, where the fatal bullet entered, was bruised and blackened.

Jim's casket was carried to the grave by pallbearers Frank Gregg, J. S. Whitsett, William Gregg, O. H. Lewis, Dr. M. C. Miller, and George Wigginton. Ten former men of Quantrill marched two abreast, preceding them.

As dirt was shoveled on Jim's grave, one of his sisters said, "Poor Jim. He wanted to come back to Missouri, and he had to kill himself to have his heart yearnings gratified."

That the content of Jim's letters and recollections by Cora Lee McNeil and her daughter Deedee should be made known so many years after Jim's death gives us pause. Although Jim claimed that through these letters he was telling the truth, we can see that wasn't always so. His reasons for altering the truth would be only known to him.

And who are we to believe truly held Jim's heart, Cora Lee or Alix? Did Jim allow Alix to reenter his life after his loss of Cora Lee? Did Alix indeed have letters from Jim that she was going to make public? If so, they have never surfaced. The true story of the love he held so dearly, whether Cora Lee or Alix, may never be revealed.

In the end, Jim Younger remains an enigma.

POEMS BY JIM YOUNGER

"Con Amour" With Love
James H. Younger
June 1897
Stillwater, Minnesota

If I should one day wander
O'er the Plaines of Deva Chan,
Ask me not to pause or ponder,
Ask me not its scenes to scan.
Till I feel your arms about me,
Once again feel thrills of bliss,
For I would not know 'twas Heaven,
If they robbed me of your kiss.
Thus I say I now surrender,
Heart to heart we stand as one,
Care I not for earth born splendor,
Care I not for cheering sun.
I believed love was denied me,
Or was slain by Sorrow's dart,
Lo a voice now whispers softly,
"Evermore, my own Sweetheart."

"The Raytown Road"
Jim Younger
1890

"Why do I love it, you ask me today?
That smooth white road with its winding way,
That stretches afar over hill and dale
Anon peeps out the shadowy vale.
Why do I love it? Because it was there,
I found love hidden—ah, she was fair!
As she sat in the moonlights silica sheen,
While Cupid shot from his bow as arrow keen.

'Twas a mid-summer night, the air was sweet,
With the breath of bloom, the scene complete.
In creative art and there I bestowed
My heart's great love, on the Raytown Road.
The fragrant breeze ever whispers to me
Of a woman whose love is as deep as the sea,
And I marvel such angles have earthly abode,
I loved her and kissed her, on the Raytown Road.

Then love grew bolder and asked for more
Having found the key to the sacred door,
And I whispered softly, "Joy of my life
I must have thee, hold thee, for aye, as my wife."
The stars twinkled shyly, the birds in their glee
Warbled the answer to their mates in the trees
My arms stole about her, Oh! I was bold—
Thus I wooed her and kissed her, on the Raytown Road.

SOURCES

THE AUTHOR HAS STUDIED THE YOUNGER FAMILY OVER FORTY YEARS
and in some instances relied on her accumulated knowledge of
the character of James and Cole Younger. She also referenced her
own trilogy of books *The Outlaw Youngers: A Confederate Brotherhood* (Madison Books, 1992), *Outlaws: The Illustrated History of the
James-Younger Gang* (Elliott & Clark, 1997), and *Jesse James: The
Man and the Myth* (Berkley Books, 1998).

BOOKS

Appler, Augustus C., *The Life, Character and Daring Exploits of the
  Younger Brothers* (Eureka Publishing Company, 1876)
Bronaugh, W. C., *The Youngers Fight for Freedom* (E. W. Stephens, 1906)
Bryan, William S., and Rose, Robert, *A History of the Pioneer Families of
  Missouri* (1876)
Cantrell, Dallas, *Youngers Fatal Blunder* (Naylor, 1973)
Connolly, William E., *Quantrill and the Border Wars* (Torch Press, 1910)
Croy, Homer, *Last of the Great Outlaws* (Duell, Sloan and Pearce, 1956)
Cummins, Jim, *Jim Cummins the Guerilla* (1908)
Hale, Donald, *They Rode with Quantrill (1982)*
Helbron, W. C., *Convict Life at the Minnesota State Prison* (W. C.
  Helbron, 1909)
History of Jackson County (Union History Co., 1888)
History of Paso Robles (California Historical Press)
History of San Luis Obispo (California Historical Press)
McNeill, Cora, *Mizzoura* (Mizzoura Publishing Company, 1898)
Miller, Rick, *Bounty Hunter* (Creative, 1988)
Settle, William. A. Jr., *Cole Younger Writes to Lizzie Daniel* (1987)
Settle, William A. Jr., *Jesse James Was His Name* (Bison Books, 1977)

Yeatman, Ted, *Frank and Jesse James, The Story behind the Legend* (Cumberland House, 2003)
Younger, Cole, *Cole Younger by Himself* (The Henneberry Co., 1903)
Zink, Wilbur, *The Roscoe Gun Battle* (Democrat, 1982)

CORRESPONDENCE

A. C. Green to Henry Wolfer, July 13, 1901
Alix J. Muller to Governor Van Sant, January 8, 1902
Andrew Schoch to Henry Wolfer, July 1901
Ardyce Twyman Haukenberry to Josephine Green, April 19, 1926
B. G. Yates to W. C. Bronaugh, February 27, 1889
Bob Younger to "Aunt," January 25, 1883
Bob Younger to Mrs. McGill, Easter 1887
C. N. Beandoorz to Henry Wolfer, December 17, 1912
C. R. Graves to Henry Wolfer, December 17, 1912
Claude Bronaugh to Author, June 24, 1983
Cole Younger to J. W. Buel, October 31, 1880
Cole Younger to Fannie Twyman, April 26, 1885
Cole Younger to W. C. Bronaugh, March 19, 1891
Cole Younger to W. R. Marshal, January 18, 1894
Cole Younger to Henry Wolfer, September 20, 1901; October 21, 1901;
    February 22, 1902; November 14, 1904
Cole Younger to Lizzie Daniel, 1901
Cole Younger to Harry Hoffman, April 4, 1907; March 7, 1916
Cole Younger to Dr. M. E. Withrow, February 24, 1915
Cole Younger to N. L. Horton, February 14 (year unknown)
Cora Deming W. C. Bronaugh, November 1, 1897
Correspondence of Bob Younger to "Aunt," 1877–1888
Correspondence of Jim Younger, 1899–1901
Deedee Deane to Wilbur Zink, 1966–1968
Delores Reed Fozzard to Author, October 12, 1986
Donald E. Lambkin to Author, November 7, 1986
Donald Hale to Author, June 8, 1983
Dr. M. E. Withrow to Frank Hall, April 30, 1947
F. A. Whittier to Henry Wolfer, September 29, 1902
F. A. Whittier to J. A. Lawrence, June 18, 1924
F. M. Rawlins to Author, January 3, 1986
Frank James to W. C. Bronaugh, February 19, 1903
George M. Bennett to Henry Wolfer, July 19, 1903; July 22, 1901
Harry Hoffman to B. J. George, June 3, 1958; June 25, 1958; undated

Harry Younger Hall to Henry Wolfer, November 14, 1904
Henry H. Sibley to W. C. Bronaugh, July 8, 1889
Henry Wolfer to P. N. Peterson, August 16, 1901
Henry Wolfer to Jim Younger, October 24, 1901
Henry Wolfer to F. A. Whittier, September 3, 1903
Henry Wolfer to J. G. Maertin, February 1, 1904
Henry Wolfer to Cole Younger, February 9, 1905
J. H. Schurmeier to Henry Wolfer, July 12, 1901
Jack Hall to Author, 1984
James Elwin to Henry Wolfer, July 10, 1901
Jim Younger to Cora Lee McNeill Deming, 1901–1902
Jim Younger to Henry Wolfer, August, 14, 1901; August 26, 1901;
	September 1, 1901; October 21, 1901; November 15, 1901;
	November 25, 1901; June 26, 1902; August 20, 1902; August 24, 1902
Jim Younger to Lizzie Daniel, 1901
John Mills to Author, November 3, 1982; December 6, 1982
John Wilson to "My Dear Sallie," date unknown
Lee Smith to Author, May 18, 1983
Leola Mayes to Author, December 13, 1983; February 29, 1984;
	April 17, 1984
Mildred Addy to Author, November 1, 1983
Mrs. Frank Hall to Dr. M. E. Withrow, December 3, 1915. N. O. Tate to
	Henry Wolfer, July 15, 1901
P. N. Peterson to Henry Wolfer, August 19, 1901
R. W. McClaugary to Henry Wolfer, May 30, 1908
Ted Yeatman to Author, over 50 letters from 1981 to 2003
Retta Younger to W. C. Bronaugh, September 22, 1891
Retta Younger to Peter Freligh, September 23, 1891
W. F. Wiggins to Henry Wolfer, September 22, 1903

INTERVIEWS

*Most of these interviews were conducted between 1980 and 1987
Members of the Younger family, including:

Le Annis Fox (cousin)
Lena Younger Gilpin (cousin)
Carolyn Hall (Hall family)
Jack Hall (Hall family)
Leola Mayes (Duncan family)

Delores Fozzard Reed (Kelley family)
Donna Rose Harrell (Rose family)
Lee Smith (Hall family)
William Talley (Talley family)
Zudora Von Demfange (Duncan family)
Dorothy Ward (Duncan family)
Ruth Whipple (Duncan family)
Harriet Wickstrom (Duncan Family)
Dreat Younger (cousin)
Notes were used from an interview of Minnie Padgett (Duncan family)
    conducted by Elizabeth George on October 28, 1959
Betty Barr (great-granddaughter of Jesse James)
Thelma Barr (granddaughter of Jesse James by marriage)
Ruth Coder Fitzgerald (family of Clell Miller)
C. E. Miller (family of Clell Miller)
Milton Perry (James historian)
John Nicholson (great-nephew of Jesse James)
Ethelrose James Owens (granddaughter of Jesse James)
James R. Ross (great-grandson of Jesse James)
Dr. William A. Settle (James historian)
Florence Wiley (great-granddaughter of Pearl Starr Reed
Ted Yeatman (James historian)

ARTICLES AND PAMPHLETS

"A Terrible Quintet," *The Kansas City Star*, John Newman Edwards,
    1875
"Edward Noonan Interviewed," *Mankato Spotlight*, date unknown
"*The Families of Charles Lee and Henry Washington Younger: A Genealogical
    Sketch*," Marley Brant, 1986
"The Gettysburg of the James-Younger Gang," *The Southern Minnesotan*
"Historical Bank Raid Centered on Ames Family," by Bob Warn for the
    Northfield Historical Society, 1977
"The Jesse James Robbery," Adair, Iowa pamphlet
"The Miller Family," Ruth Coder Fitzgerald, *James Farm Journal*, 1988
"Northfield Bank Robbery," Northfield Historical Society
"Quantrill, James, Younger et al. Leadership in a Guerilla Movement,
    Missouri, 1861–1865," Don R. Bowman, *Military Affairs*, Vol. XLI,
    No. 1, February 1977

SOURCES

San Luis County Pathways, New Paradigm Press, 1981
"Three Years with Quantrill," John McCorkle, Armstrong, MO,
Herald, 1914

UNPUBLISHED MANUSCRIPTS

Cole Younger by Harry Younger Hall (undated)
Interview with Bob Younger by George Craig (1886)
"The Youngers Last Stand," Harry C. Hoffman
"The Fog amidst the Rumors Cleared Away," Harry Hoffman

RECORDS

1850 Jackson County Census
1860 Cass County Census
Affidavit of Frank J. Wilcox, September 1876
Affidavit of G. E. Hobbs, September 1876
Affidavit of J. S. Allen, September 1876
Clelland Miller Trial Transcript, Iowa 1871
Complaint, Northfield Robbery, 1876
Coroner's Inquest into the Deaths of John Younger and Edwin Daniels,
    Testimony of Theodrick Snuffer, W. J. Allen, and G. W. McDonald
Coroner's Report of John Younger and J. S. Allen, 1874
Death Certificate of James H. Younger
Employment Request by Andrew Schoch, 1901
Employment Certificate, Jim Younger by Andrew Schoch, 1902
Indictment against T. C. James and Robert Younger for the Northfield
    Robbery and Murders, 1876
Land Title Issued to James H. Younger, Texas
Life Prisoner Roll, Stillwater Prison
National Archive Military Record of Coleman Younger
National Archives Military Record of Irvin Walley
Ninth United States Census, 1870, Dallas County, Texas
Pardon Petition, Missouri Legislature, 1899
Parole Papers of James Younger, 1901
Parole Reports of Cole Younger (monthly), August 1901 to January 1903
Parole Reports of Jim Younger (monthly), August 1901 to
    September 1902
Resolution of Pardon of T. C. Younger and James Younger, 1901
St. Paul City Directory, 1901

193

Statement of Cole Younger in regard to the Stillwater Prison Fire, 1884
Warrant of Arrest, T. C. James and Robert Younger, 1876

PERSONAL ACCOUNTS
Charles Armstrong, Madelia, Minnesota, 1945
Cole Younger to Harry Hoffman, 1914
G. M. Palmer, Mankato, Minnesota, 1938
Hiram George, 1900
Leva Hull Thomas (undated)
"My Twelve Years with Cole Younger" Todd George
Robert E. Younger, 1885
Statement of Cole Younger to Harry Hoffman (1914)
"The Life of Mrs. Frances Twyman by Herself," 1901
The Scrapbook of Hardin Hall

NEWSPAPERS
*Some of these articles were preserved in scrapbooks and the dates
and titles were not included.

Appleton City Tribune, September 22, 1903
Chicago Herald, Jack Lair, March 24, 1916
Daily Missouri Democrat, September 1, 1863
Kansas City Star, "A Visit to the Youngers," 1901
Kansas City Times, "Interview with Cora McNeill Deming," 1897;
    "Doctor Recalls Younger Brothers as Men above the
    Outlaw Class," October 24, 1958
Lee's Summit Journal, February 20, 1903; March 23, 1916
Lee's Summit Ledger, March 25, 1874
Madelia Times Messenger, "The Inside Story of the Northfield Bank
    Robbery," March 27, 1936
Mankato Free Press, "The Younger Gang Comes to Mankato,"
    December 1876
Minneapolis Tribune, September 8, 1876
Faribault newspaper, "Northfield Bank Robbery Is Recalled by Jail
    Guard's *Son*" *(date unknown)*
Norton (Kansas) Champion, "One Night with Jim Younger" (date
    unknown)

St. Clair County Democrat, June 26, 1911; December 14, 1911; August 28, 1913

St. Louis Republican, August 3, 1902

St. Paul Pioneer Press, "Convicts Armed as Prison Burns" (date unknown), September, 1876; 1889; "Held Fast in Prison," July 13, 1897; July 14, 1897; July 11, 1901; "Youngers Stop Friendly Move," June, 1902; April 2, 1909

Stillwater Evening Gazette, July 12, 1901

The Southern Minnesotan (date unknown)

Washington Post, December 6, 1903

Index

ABOUT THE AUTHOR

MARLEY BRANT IS THE AUTHOR OF TEN BOOKS, BOTH FICTION AND nonfiction. Her books have been featured in *People* magazine, the *New York Times*, and numerous other newspapers; have been the basis for television programs on A&E and VH1; and have served as the primary research for hours of television programming on the History Channel, PBS, TBS, and CMT. Brant was the cocreator and coproducer of the "Outlaws, Rebels and Rogues" episode of the TBS special *The Untold West*. Brant has been employed in the entertainment industry as a biographical writer, music and television producer, publicist, and artist development executive. She is the author of nine nonfiction books about outlaws, television, and rock music. Brant's books *The Outlaw Youngers: A Confederate Brotherhood* and *Jesse James: The Man and the Myth* were both recognized with the Milton F. Perry Award for extensive research and contribution to American history.

CPSIA information can be obtained
at www.ICGtesting.com
Printed in the USA
BVHW072053230421
605723BV00001B/1